Songs of the Soul

To Patricia —

Listen to the songs within your soul.

Anne Candell

Songs of the Soul

Library of Congress Catalog Card Number 96-60622

ISBN 0-9652504-0-7

Manufactured in the United States of America
First Printing 1996
Second Printing 1996

Published by

⊞ VERITAS PRESS Ltd.
PO Box 270735
West Hartford CT 06127-0735

Produced by
PPC BOOKS
Westport CT

Songs of the Soul

Anne Carroll Decker

 VERITAS PRESS Ltd.

Prelude to the Angels

One

The Beginning

This story started about thirty years ago, when I saw an angel.

Each summer, my aunts rented a house at the ocean. The living room was decorated with a couch, a few chairs, and a fireplace which blocked the view of the sea. I was the only child in the room and uninterested in the adults' conversation. Who would be, with a radiant winged angel to play with?

At my side, stood a tall, beautifully dressed creature. He was much larger than I, robed in golden clothes and almost transparent in appearance. He remained silent, but I felt his benevolence. Although years have passed, I can still see the room and him quite clearly. His face was angular and masculine, but soft in expression. Blonde hair cascaded to his shoulders, almost touching the hinge of his massive wings. The color of the wings flickered in comforting golden hues.

Always a polite child, I jumped from the couch and began dragging a large wicker chair closer to where I had been sitting.

"What are you doing?" someone asked.

"Getting a chair for my Guardian Angel," I answered simply.

Naturally, everyone began to laugh.

That was the last time I saw him for many years. Children may indulge in "imaginary friends," but adults with similar experiences are placed under psychiatric care.

But, unlike a salesman who will finally leave your door and go bang on someone else's, God does not leave. He remains, patient and loving, waiting for you to eventually listen to His call.

By age thirty-seven, the knocking became too incessant for me to ignore. I had to open the door. In the interim period from my childhood to this age, I occasionally had glimpses of angels and flashes of intuition, but I dismissed them.

Yet, there were always a few events which I couldn't explain—one of which occurred when I was a senior in college. On a cold, spring evening, I left the library and headed back toward my dormitory. The walkway I chose, which ended at a major campus intersection, was well lit and usually well traveled. But that evening I found myself alone on the path. As I descended the Hill, with the busy street below me, an inner voice said, quite clearly, "Let them pass." Abruptly, I stopped.

Through the iron gates which encircled the upper campus, I saw two men walking toward the intersection. This was not unusual at the university, where hundreds of

2

students and teachers from various countries constantly moved between buildings. If I had continued at my regular pace, our paths would have crossed within a matter of minutes. Thinking I was being paranoid, I nevertheless heeded the instruction. Standing still, I watched the tall, white man and the short, black man disappear from view.

Later, as I opened the door to my dormitory, a crowd had gathered in the lobby. "A girl on campus has been attacked," the resident assistant announced to the group. "By two men."

"One is a tall, white man," she continued, "His companion is shorter and black."

Although I've had other such experiences, most not as powerful, I tried to close my mind to them. I explained them away as fatigue, an active imagination, or any excuse I could find. Nor was I ever willing to share these experiences with anyone...afraid people would laugh.

Or worse, they'd think I was crazy.

Up until recently, I would have been the first to agree with them. Quite frankly, I thought people who experienced such phenomena were delusional. They must want to believe in apparitions so desperately that they dreamed them up.

But now, what happened to me after I "opened the door" seems to me—if not exactly normal—surely the most sensible part of my life. Undoubtedly, some will ridicule this story and I understand such skepticism. To them, I can only say, this is my experience.

And it has changed my life.

Two

Opening the Door

"Call to me and I will answer you; I will tell you wonderful and marvelous things that you know nothing about." Jeremiah 33:3

Mid-March

The nightmares were frequent. They were so disturbing in fact, that I talked to a friend of mine, a minister, and asked his advice. "Go through them," he said. "Go past them. Don't let the fear stop you from the message." Easier said than done. He didn't dream of monstrous, snarling goats forcing their way into his kitchen. At 5'2" and 110 pounds, I struggled vainly to block their stampede. No matter how desperately I tried to awake, the goats grew in magnitude, overtaking my house, spewing horrendous bile from their mouths. Who in his right mind would want to confront these beasts?

My friend knew me too well. Anytime I encountered

something different—frightening or fantastic—I would block it out. Why did I need to learn any spiritual lessons? From catechism class, I had learned the basics: There are Ten Commandments. Obey them. There are Seven Deadly Sins. Avoid them. If a person followed these edicts, upon death, he would probably enter Purgatory, and eventually, ascend to Heaven. What else did I need to know?

Obviously, *plenty.*

My husband and I had signed up for a day retreat in Madison, Connecticut. Although I am Catholic and my husband is Congregationalist, we've never had a problem understanding each other's faiths. The retreat, a day of instruction and prayer, was offered at a Catholic retreat center by a Congregationalist minister. It seemed designed for us. As we drove through the seaside town that morning, we discovered that neither of us wanted to attend the retreat. We had enrolled for each other.

March's freezing snow wrapped around us as we trudged toward the Retreat House. Although I longed for another cup of coffee and my warm bed forty miles away, as chance—or more accurately, God—would have it, the day would become a turning point in my life.

The ocean had always been important to me. Somehow whenever I was within sight or smell of the sea, I felt better. Calmer, more at peace with myself. Just at home. Perhaps this comes from growing up near the Rhode Island beaches. The topic for the retreat had something to do with music and prayer. Because both my husband and I lack musical ability and are unable to carry even the most familiar of tunes, we felt lost among the participants. But, as the music in the background played, I closed my eyes, heard the

crashing waves, and thought of God.

I don't know how God comes to other people. Perhaps through simple kindness, through divine intervention, through tender, selfless prayers. But that day, He came quietly to me. In essence, I heard, "Open the door to my knock. Listen to my voice. Talk to me. Do not be afraid."

Fear is an incredibly strong emotion. It blocked me from prayer, myself and God. Whenever I stepped closer to the fear, my head ached and the muscles in my chest fluttered. Soon, these flutterings turned into all-out palpitations. It was easier to stay away. "I am doing the best I can, Lord," I said. "Please, let me be." Deep within me, I realized the excuse was no longer working. I had to relinquish the fear and put my faith in God.

Easier said than done.

Throughout the retreat, as we listened to a variety of music, from Gospel to Handel, I knew something was changing within me.

That night, I dreamed of the gnarring goats. This time, rather than barricading my kitchen door, I threw it open, allowing the monstrous creatures to run into my home—trampling past me. As I steadied myself against the wall, I gathered my courage and faced them. A soft purring filled the room. Each goat had changed into a docile, white lamb.

Unknown to me, I had reached a turning point.

Up until that time I had measured junctures in concrete terms. Immediately upon graduation from Tufts University, I became a stockbroker at a national brokerage house. The idea of working solely on commission appealed to me—the

harder I worked, the more money I earned. By age 25, I was named the youngest vice president in the firm, one of only two females in that position. My days were spent consumed with financial matters, early morning to late evenings, including weekends. I specialized in tax shelters and easily conversed with clients investing in limited partnerships. My achievement was tangible and easily measured. I liked it that way.

During that period, I met my husband, Tom. He was fifteen years my senior and also a vice president of the firm. Although he was Protestant, divorced, and had three children—it was love at first sight. Within six months, an annulment had been granted to his first marriage and we were married in the Catholic Church.

Eventually, with the phasing out of tax shelters, I decided to move my career in a new direction. I had written a couple of unpublished thrillers and, during this last year, had been finishing a Master's Degree at Wesleyan University. I lived a normal life, working during the week, going to Church on Sunday...and praying, usually, when I needed or wanted a favor.

When I prayed, I prayed the Rosary. I felt comfortable, peaceful and safe reciting prayers which I learned as a child. I liked the feel of the wooden beads clicking through my fingers; keeping count of exactly how many Hail Mary's I completed. Fifty-three Hail Marys and six Our Fathers. Yet after the retreat in Madison, I knew I needed to expand my prayer life.

The following week, at home in the privacy of my house, I heard the call again. It wasn't a loudspeaker, but a need, deep within me to sit down and listen to the Lord. I felt like

a magnet pulled toward metal. I had a busy week planned, with no allotments for solitude. The excuses kept forming in my mind: homework, Tae Kwon Do, laundry, and grocery shopping. Regardless, I sat down.

Closing my eyes, I tried to breathe regularly. After all, didn't all the cloistered monks pray like this? Didn't all the contemplatives in religions around the world meditate? Why was I frightened and distracted?

And terrified of the silence?

I had never been taught meditation and surprised myself at how easily I entered the stillness of my mind. Once there, my throat hurt; it felt dry and parched...and even in my mind I realized my vocal chords were paralyzed with fear. In seconds, I pictured myself in an alleyway in London which I had never seen but somehow knew existed. The details of the place were precise and exact: crumbling stone steps of a church, the smell of baking bread, dampness clinging to my skin. A slight mist covered everything. I hurried down the street, past row houses and large hansom cabs, finally turning toward an even smaller alleyway.

A dilapidated bookstore, with the sign half-hanging from its doorway, was located in the basement level of a brick building. I hurried down the black iron staircase, feeling the rail's peeling paint scratch my hand and knowing that the bookstore owner waited for me.

He was an elderly man, dressed in an oversized dark cardigan, standing in the middle of this circular bookstore. A long, white beard covered most of his square face; wrinkles covered the rest. He held a large, rectangular crystal slab. Rows and rows of books jammed the shelves. The room had little lighting, only a single fixture hanging from the ceiling.

The place smelled musty and hadn't been dusted in years.

The man clutched the slab closer to his chest, nodded, and glanced toward a circular staircase. No words were exchanged, but it was clear he wanted me to descend the stairs. Although I felt propelled to continue, the fear of entering the unknown nearly suffocated me.

I began wondering if the Devil or something Evil, was trying to influence me. I considered fleeing.

That was what I had always done, but this time I continued on my journey. I felt terrified but prayed aloud, constantly asking if this was for the greater good.

After descending the second staircase, I walked into a large room. The walls were crystal, not unlike the slab which the bookstore owner had been holding. The place shone with bright, white light; prisms of light reflected off the crystal.

A man in white robes appeared.

My heart pounded wildly and the muscles in my chest seemed to expand and contract—all the classic signs of a panic attack. I wanted to run, but felt as if my feet were anchored to the crystal floor.

Swallowing hard, I finally found my voice. I asked, "Are you for the good?" It may sound like a foolish question to some, but I had no intention of getting involved with any being—human or spiritual—who was not there for the goodness of my soul.

Before me, his face turned Satanic, angelic, and again Satanic. Remembering the gnarring goats, I stood firm. "If this is for the good of my soul, Lord, help me to stay on this journey," I said adamantly.

The horrible face disappeared, and the man in the white

robe remained with me. My throat no longer hurt, but my chest still ached. Barely able to open my mouth, I asked for guidance.

His beautiful face and dark brown eyes, conveyed both knowledge and comfort. His skin was smooth, but as he smiled, fine lines formed around his eyes, making his smile even more human.

He began communicating at once. "You are a part of everyone," he said. "The most important lessons are Love and Unity."

"Unity?" I asked.

He nodded. "You were all one. You are to love your neighbor as yourself. You are mirrored in each other. Every condemning word said ricochets back to you."

I became angry, and my chest hurt even more. This was not the message I wanted. Adamantly, I answered him back. "During the evening news, I saw a clip about a group of people in New Haven who had sexually abused a three-year-old girl. Their actions don't reflect mine."

His voice flowed on like a quiet river. Powerful. "That is their choice. Their choices are their own. God has not condemned them, they have condemned themselves. And if you pray for them, they can be brought back to Him."

"I don't want to pray for them," I answered back.

His voice remained still, showing no surprise. "All energy which you release, returns. Goodness returns, as does evil. You must relinquish your judgment. God does not judge."

"He does at Judgment Day," I said, correcting him.

"These people have already judged themselves," he said. "By choosing to turn from the Light, they are in darkness.

But, you can help them find the Light. Through prayer for them. Through prayer for yourself."

The serenity of his words were powerful; then he added, simply, "You are all one."

This was not a message I wanted to hear. "Why are you telling me this?" I asked.

"Write it down. Transcribe it."

"I don't want that responsibility," I said. "What if I'm making this up? What if these messages are wrong?"

"You can never be wrong if it is for the greatest good," he concluded.

Upon opening my eyes, I realized that this inner vision had ended. Looking around my family room, everything seemed exactly as it had been.

Except for me.

Desperately needing some advice, or perhaps something to validate my sanity, I turned to the Bible. I rarely read it, and it opened randomly to Jeremiah, the negative prophet. Here was a man after my own heart: he didn't want any holy messages and sometimes argued with God. My eyes fell to this passage: "Go and find Jeremiah and take good care of him. Do not harm him but do for him whatever he wants."

It gave me peace.

The Angels and Their Gifts

Three

Patience and Grace

The next day the call became stronger. As I sipped my morning coffee, I tried to ignore it. "Yesterday was just an anomaly," I told myself. "Something to tuck into the recess of my mind and forget about." But God is persistent, His call commanding. The call pushed like a wind, forcing me to walk in a different direction. Like the wind, its strength was invisible to the naked eye, but clearly powerful.

The family room where I had begun my prayer, faced a pond. Large windows allowed the morning sun to filter through, warming my face. Each morning after watching part of a morning talk show, I found myself turning the television off. Although I had lots of things to do—besides my thesis, and a brunch for thirty-five people in our home—there was no choice but to sit down and listen to this force. Although I heard the call, I wanted, *desperately,* to ignore it.

Settling on the couch, my Rottweiler panting heavily in the corner, I closed my eyes. Again, I found myself hurrying

through the London street, down the staircase, and into another room. Fear began to engulf me as I tumbled down a crystal tunnel.

Even as it happened, I found it difficult to believe. Although I was semi-aware of sitting in my family room, another part of me was vividly exiting the tunnel.

Alone, on a white stretch of beach, stood an Archangel. His presence felt familiar. Even from a distance, I saw that he was tall—at least three times my height—and in his right hand he held a large, golden staff. On top of this hooked staff was a cross, tilted slightly, resembling an x. The x was encrusted with an array of jewels. His presence was formidable. Standing in the warm sand, I felt insignificant and small.

He called to me.

I stayed still. His massive presence seemed too extraordinary for me to grasp. Answering his greeting, I said loudly, "I think you've picked the wrong person." I wanted to return to the safety of my home, return to its comfort.

Initially, he did not reply, but then his voice became stern. "You are here to learn and accept the gifts of God. You can no longer leave."

"What gifts?" I asked, scanning the area around him. But my curiosity wasn't enough to convince me to stay. Informing him that I was reluctant, I pleaded, "Please go visit someone else. Someone who will be delighted to see you."

Seconds later, I found myself at his side. We sat on a large rock, which jutted out to sea. The Archangel opened his staff, allowing the contents to fall. Thousands of diamonds, small and large, cascaded from the inside of the

golden-lined pole. They covered the rock and sand surrounding us.

"Please accept a gift," he said, pointing toward the gems.

I reached down, picked up a diamond and dropped it immediately. The heat from the stone burned my hand.

"It is the energy of the gift," he said, his voice commanding, yet kind. "Hold it and eventually the energy will no longer burn you. It will become one with your body. It is as divine as you are."

Tentatively, I picked up another gem. This time it did not burn.

"This," he said, indicating the small stone in my hand, "is Patience."

"Patience?"

He nodded. "You must open yourself to God's blessing of Patience. Most importantly, it is patience for others, then patience for yourself. It is imperative that you have patience for each other. The way God has patience for you."

He explained that the angels had been waiting for me. "You have been like an inchworm crossing eternity."

The words crushed me—*an inchworm crossing eternity*. I slid from the rock, crumpled into the warm sand and cried.

The Archangel's demeanor softened as he bent and touched me. His large hands held mine. "Do not fear, this is your journey. Even the inchworm will reach God, as will you. God is eternity. We have been patient with you, as you must be with mankind. You must open up your divinity and accept God's gift of Patience." With a sweep of his hand, he indicated the glistening diamonds. "These are God's gifts waiting for each of you. They surround you all the time, yet few are willing to accept them." He added matter-of-factly,

17

"It is a human condition."

From Biblical reading, I assumed an angelic visit would bring me peace and contentment. But rather, I felt uneasy and inadequate. "I'd rather not hear anything else."

"It is too late for that," the Archangel said. "With God, all things are possible and you are ready to learn, receive, accept and practice these gifts."

This creature hadn't understood me; he had the *wrong* woman. I explained my dilemma. "Last night on the news, I heard a story about a murderer. I tried praying for him, but God must realize my prayers weren't genuine." In the depths of my heart, I had hoped someone would kill the criminal.

"That is why the gift of Patience needs to be accepted," the Archangel said quietly.

He handed me another diamond. I was surprised it was not hot.

"Here is the gift of Grace. You will need it for your journey," he said.

Shaking my head in astonishment, I held the stone. This whole experience was overwhelming. "Why am I getting these messages?" I asked. "Are they spiritual visions, or am I imagining everything?" Opening the palm of my hand, I let the bright sunlight shine on the diamond. Dozens of fragments of brilliant light reflected into the air.

"I am one of the largest angels," he said humbly. "I was sent to you because you are reluctant and difficult. Some people get smaller and lesser angels, because they are more willing, and easier to lead." He paused, then added, "God has sent me to help you with these lessons. You cannot turn back—you know this."

Sensing my hesitancy, he said, "We will discuss this further, and you will accept the gifts as you need them."

"I must go," I said, biting on my lower lip. I could not listen any longer.

He did not appear surprised. "Someday, I promise you, you will not feel any barriers to this message. You will accept your divinity and the divinity of others with joy and not fear. That is your pathway."

He continued, even though I didn't want to hear more. "These gifts are as multitudinous as the grains of sands on a beach. They surround everyone." He again swept his hand in the air. "Can you not see them? They surround you entirely, so much so they almost suffocate you. Yet, people are reluctant. Each of you has formed a shell around your souls, an armor from the Lord who loves you so much."

I half-listened, and half-wondered, about my sanity.

He continued. "You must open your heart and spirit and let the breath of God come into your soul. He is everywhere, as are His gifts. The gifts are many; they are there for the taking. You must be open to these spiritual gifts."

None of this was helping ease my fears or tensions. "Even if I could accept these gifts," I said, "How will I apply them?"

"The gifts will guide you on your path. God will hold His hand out to you. You must tell everyone that these gifts hover around them, all the time, waiting to be requested."

"And you?" I asked.

He nodded. "We have been knocking loudly on your door, as we do everyone's. But, like a house with the music too loud, and the voices too argumentative, no one can hear the visitors. We continue to knock, louder and louder, but

humanity turns up its selfish noise." He smiled at me, a tender, warm smile, which helped ease my fears. "With answering the door, comes responsibility."

Oh, my.

"When you are quiet, and still, you can hear the knock—faint or strong. And then, it is up to you to answer the door. Ask, and you shall seek. Seek your journey. God is always at the door, waiting for humanity to open it."

The Archangel paused as I closed my fingers tightly around the gem. "Tell the others to open the door, reach out for the gifts, accept His love and their own divinity, and the journey will begin. A peace will prevail within you."

I wondered aloud. "Journey?" I didn't know I was about to embark on one. Although I had read about the peace of God, I never thought much about it. That was for the religious, or saints, or people who were more willing to sacrifice than I. Where would this journey take me? And was *I* willing to go?

Resting against the rock, I tried to let the Archangel's words sink in. He didn't give me time to think.

"You have seen me before," he said.

Agreeing with him, I recalled the time at another retreat when he had appeared within my mind.

"Not that time," he said quite firmly, shaking his head. "When you were small..."

"...and I pulled out a chair for you," I said, finishing his sentence. My voice trembled, remembering the incident. With the passing of years, I had assumed that the visit was no more than a childhood fantasy. "Everyone laughed. So then, I closed my eyes to you."

The Archangel smiled benevolently. "Why were you so

certain it was imaginary? Until you were told it was impossible, you were willing to accept the divine as common. Why is it impossible now?"

"Because," I explained slowly, emphasizing each word. "People think you're crazy. It's okay for a six-year-old, but not for an adult."

"People must learn to nourish the children," the Archangel said sadly. "They are wholly divine. Their souls have not been buried. They see more than the adults. Which makes the adults frightened and jealous."

After he finished, we sat silently on the beach. His voice was soft and kind: "I was with you then. I am with you now. I have always been with you."

Four

Serenity

As I awakened each day, something or someone urged me to seek the silence and pray. Many times in my life, usually at the most strife-filled moments, I prayed—but this was different. The comfort I found in saying prayers such as the Hail Mary or the Our Father, was not appearing with these meditations. Instead, something profound was happening; I found myself saying, quick brief prayers for complete strangers.

And, quite frankly, it surprised me.

On the third day of this journey, I kissed my husband good-bye, straightened up the house, and gathered papers together for my thesis. I had no time that day to "pray." The sessions had been relatively short—less than twenty minutes each—but immediately afterwards, I transcribed my memories onto the computer. In total, the process consumed an hour and a half. Yet, deep within me, I realized that the excuse of "no time" was only that—an excuse. In reality, I

did not want to confront anything out of the ordinary.

But the urge to pray was strong. I soon found myself sitting in the family room. The pond was exceptionally peaceful. During the spring, the honking of Canadian geese reverberates through the house. But this day, as I closed my eyes, all the sounds and sights which brought me comfort disappeared.

With my eyes closed, and my feet tucked beneath my knees, my mind quickly took me to the same alleyway, bookstore and staircases.

As I descended the stairs, I entered a large, dark library. The bindings on the books were a mixture of gold and dusty leather. The Archangel stood among the racks, waiting for me. As usual, his robes were flowing and golden. The material did not seem earthly; it threw off a warm glow, an illumination. Fear began to engulf me; this one even stronger than the others. I stood in front of the Archangel, crooking my neck upwards, and said, "I'm really sorry, but you've picked the wrong person for these visits." My voice quivered as I added, "I'm scared and frightened."

Gently, he handed me another diamond. "The stone of Serenity," he said softly. "Hold it against your chest, it will help you."

Unlike yesterday's gift, it did not burn, but felt warm against my body. I pressed it against my breast, drawing comfort from its heat.

He sighed, staring directly into my eyes. "You are a difficult case."

"Then, please," I implored, "Go somewhere else."

He answered firmly. "We have no choice. It is your time. You have heard your call."

Looking back on his words, I wished I had pursued them further. Instead, I questioned him about that day's lesson.

The tone of the Archangel's voice contained a rich mixture of wisdom and kindness. He spoke calmly. "Each of you is born mostly spirit," he said. "Your soul is here to learn from your earthly experience. Yet, as the years progress, a shell of fear and desperation forms around your body."

"A shell?"

"Yes," he said, pointing to me. I looked down and saw a transparent, milky shell which completely encased my body. Touching it, it resembled a clear, hard plastic; a plastic which had become scratched and white through the years.

"What is this?" I asked, wondering how I had missed noticing such a shield.

The Archangel's head bowed slightly, before answering. "It is what you have done to your spirit. You have tried to squelch it, and set up an armor around it." He reached out and tapped the shell. "It is almost impenetrable. If we cannot get to your soul, the gifts cannot be accepted. This encasement suffocates both your body and soul."

I breathed in deeper, assuring myself that my lungs worked. "What do you mean, suffocates my body?"

"Touch it again," he instructed.

Running my hand down the front of my chest, I felt the rock-hard material.

"Your body cannot breathe with this," he told me again. "You are spirit and body. Yet, each day your spirit suffocates with this blockade." He stepped away, and walked down a corridor of books. "Children are born, and they are mostly spirit. They are open to receive and give love. As they grow,

with the hurt and pain of the world, they set up this invisible defense." He nodded toward mine. "As you grow older, the shell becomes thicker and tougher. Finally, accepting the gifts which surround you becomes more and more difficult. As this occurs, your body also suffocates."

He continued speaking, although he had stopped walking. His hand rested on a bookshelf. He turned away from me, yet I heard sadness in his voice. "Your body should be able to survive for hundreds of years. But each of you kills it with your armor. You believe you are protecting yourselves, but in essence, you are killing yourselves with fear." Facing me, he added, "Fear breeds hate, hate breeds death. You must dismantle this armor."

"This doesn't apply to me," I answered quickly. "I might have moments of jealousy or hatred, but I'm not a *really* bad person...I'm human, but I'm not consumed with hate."

He shook his head, as if in disbelief. "But you have seen this armor," he said. "It is not for you to measure the amount of evil. You must allow this armor to crack, so that the gifts can be accepted. Open the knowledge within yourself. These gifts are necessary to the soul, but you, in this fearful state, can't recognize them."

The stacks and stacks of books seemed oppressive—as if an overwhelming amount of knowledge waited for me. The room grew dimmer, and I longed for an open window and a cool rush of air against my face.

"Acceptance is the key," the Archangel said. "You must accept the gifts of God, acknowledge the divinity within you, and allow these gifts to meet with the divinity. The armor must be broken."

"It's easy for you to say," I retorted. After all, *he* didn't

live in a body, didn't know the bodily concerns that capture all of us. "There's disease, murders, shootings...isn't it important to guard our bodies, too?"

He smiled gently, as if speaking to a small, impatient child. "Your spirits are in bodies to learn lessons," he said. "But you cannot learn without the knowledge of the soul. In your fear, in order to maintain your bodies, you have suffocated your souls. You must allow the soul to be first, and then the body will be free."

None of this made any sense. "Free?" I asked. "Horrendous things are occurring in the world. Can't you lecture me on Sin and Judgment? Religious concepts I feel comfortable with?" I wanted him to explain morality in black and white terms—with no ambiguous gray area.

He continued smiling, as if expecting that response. "I have not contradicted your beliefs. There is a Judgment. Each of you judges yourself. There is Evil Incarnate, there is the Devil and Hell. Everyone can be called by this Evil, it is up to man to turn from the darkness. God is the light, He gives you freedom of choice. That choice is either to stay in the light or turn from Him, and thus enter the darkness. By doing either you judge yourselves."

"Then are people condemned?" I asked.

"God, who is eternal love, does not condemn. The people who have turned away have exiled themselves."

"Well," I said, running my fingers along the leather bindings, "That's unfortunate, but it's their problem."

"No," he answered sternly. "You are all one. It is your problem, also. You must pray for them to return to the light. You must pray for their salvation. They are all God's children and everything is possible with God. Everything is possible

through prayer." Standing tall, he clasped his hands together, as they fell gently to his waist. "You must pray for your enemies, you must pray that they will turn away from Evil."

I didn't like hearing this one bit. "I realize that the Bible said to 'Love God, and Love Your Neighbor as Yourself.' The concept is wonderful, but actually applying it is much more difficult."

He didn't seem surprised by my statement. The Archangel never seemed shocked at anything I said, regardless of my arguments. "With God's love, peace and serenity are possible. There is a heaven on earth."

That sounded nice.

"First," he said softly, "You must open your soul to the gifts, to the divinity. Then, you will love yourself, because your soul is love. Once this is accomplished, it will become much easier for you to pray for others. Jesus did not say, 'Love only your *good* neighbor.' He said, 'Love your neighbor.' Everyone is your neighbor. You must pray, even more strongly, for those who turn from the light.

"You are all one. You are all children of God. You must continue to pray for the Acceptance. You must stop worrying about your bodies, about the materialism which surrounds you. It will all be cared for, if the soul is nourished."

The Archangel's words sounded sensible, but I continued to *try* to explain to him the difficulty in such a task.

He shook his head. "You must stop resisting. You are all blessed, you are children of God. But you must stop ignoring His gifts. These gifts surround each of you, they try to penetrate your bodies. If you look closely, you can see them. They are waiting to be inhaled. If these gifts were accepted,

there would be no more suffering. But you must stop being selfish, you must listen to the Spirit. Listen to the Divine. Listen to God and pray for each other."

"I can't love everyone," I protested. Ashamed, but truthful, I told him my feelings. "Knowing the truth and not being able to practice it, is already making me feel guilty and unworthy."

His voice grew tender as he touched my shoulder. "We are there for you. We are praying for you, too. With God's light, all is possible."

The whole episode became overwhelming. "What if I am making this whole thing up?" I asked, inspecting him more closely, touching the silken fabric on his sleeve. "I'll be locked up. And worse, what if my transcriptions are religiously wrong?" My fears broke through, releasing a string of questions. "I can transcribe these messages, but I cannot share them."

The Archangel waited patiently.

"Well," I said hesitantly, "perhaps I could tell my friend. He's an ordained minister ... maybe I could tell him."

"Begin there," the Archangel said. "And it will grow."

"But shouldn't I feel a peace?" I said, thinking of the comfort angels brought people in the Bible. "Well, I don't. So," I concluded, still fingering the Archangel's robe, "this entire vision must be a figment of my imagination."

"It is Divine," he said firmly. "It is within you and around you. It is there, I stress, for you to Accept. Please listen to the call, please breathe quietly among the knowledge, let it engulf you. Be free to accept it. This is just a moment in the time of eternity, a small moment. But, each is important for your salvation and growth.

"Listen to the voice you have buried. Listen to the call of God. Try to accept these words. Accept and Apply the divine which is within and around you. It will be like water to the thirsty, you will drink it in, as if never having drunk before. It will quench your thirst and make you living and whole.

"Everything else will follow."

His words sounded so right, so true. But how did I know my imagination had not gone awry?

The Archangel tried to allay my fears. "Have you ever written or remembered so accurately? Have you ever been so enraptured with the Word? If goodness results from this, and people turn toward God, you can judge your actions by their rewards. It is for the greatest good."

"Please," I begged, "I can't handle anymore. It's too much."

"No," he corrected me. "It is not too much. Each time you hear of Evil, pray for those in darkness to turn toward the Divine, turn toward God. It is of the utmost importance. You have known this for centuries, but have not always applied it. Your lessons have been slow, which is not wrong, but time is of the essence. This is the pathway now. Accept and apply, and pray for each other."

Five

Intuition: Unlock the Fear

Late March

After these visits, the Archangel's words reverberated deep within me. But still, I worried. Where were these messages coming from? Had I been imagining them? I almost wanted to believe I was, that way I could dismiss them, and my life could go on undisturbed. But some of the ideas which the Archangel divulged seemed beyond even my most gracious moments.

I took a break from prayer, blocked out the calling and urges to listen to the Archangel. Convinced that he had chosen the wrong woman, I went on with my life. As a 3rd Kub in Tae Kwon Do, I kicked and punched my opponent while visualizing an attacker. The Archangel must know how I exercised, I thought, as I threw my gym bag into the car. He should've picked an aerobics person for these messages—not someone who practiced smashing an attacker's knees with a flying side-thrust kick.

He should have picked anyone, but me.

I pushed aside all thoughts of the Archangel as I exercised. Driving home from the dojang, in the silence of my car, the message was very clear. YOU MUST PRAY EVERYDAY.

I switched on the radio.

The next morning, while I folded laundry, the words repeated themselves in my head. YOU MUST PRAY EVERYDAY.

Too worn down to ignore him any longer, I found myself again with the Archangel, back on the beach. We were perched on a high cliff, overlooking the crashing waves. The sunlight was dancing on the water, and although the water seemed turbulent, I felt profoundly calm.

The Archangel sat next to me on the cliff, his torso still towering over mine. He wore a tawny golden garment, less brilliant, but as illuminating as the other robes. He was quiet and his face was almost stern. "You must pray everyday," he said. "Prayer should not be like work, so that you vacation on weekends. As you pray, you become stronger, the messages become stronger, and the soul becomes nourished. Keep in contact with the Holy Spirit; the Spirit is always there. But if you do not pray, you lose your ability to open up. Accept." Even though his tone was adamant, I felt as if he were guiding me, never forcing me.

My feet dangled off the rock, yet I felt completely safe with the Archangel next to me. Explaining my fears, I told him that I saw a movie about the Holocaust. Shaking my head in disbelief at the Nazis' actions, I revealed that I could never pray for the Nazis. "I can't possibly find forgiveness in my heart. I'm not sure if we should." My voice barely a

whisper, I added, "I think...perhaps...you're mistaken."

"Do you really?" he asked, with a twinkle in his eye.

I hesitated, "Uh huh."

"Really?" he asked again.

By now, I was angry. "Why should anyone pray for those horrible men who gassed millions of Jews?" It sounded almost blasphemous.

The Archangel replied, "Christ did not say, 'Love only those who love you.' If humanity could reach the spiritual level where it loved everyone, there would be no evil, no fear, no hate. Prayer is the only way to achieve this.

"Unlock is the word."

"Unlock what?"

He smiled again. "All your fears. We have told you to accept and love. Accept the grace of God, unlock the hatred in your hearts."

I shook my head and tugged at my cuticles. "I'm not very good at praying for my enemy."

"So I see," he said, his voice light. "It is the most difficult concept for you. But, it is the only way to reach God. Love is the answer. God is love, you must mirror Him."

"Listen," I said, clenching my jaw, "If an intruder came into my house, I'd warn him, and then I'd shoot him. Do you understand that?"

"You must pray for him."

"Where have you been?" I screamed, throwing up my hands in disgust. I pointed toward the beach. "This is the world, not heaven. If I took time to pray for an intruder, he'd harm me first."

"You must pray for him," the Archangel repeated emphatically. "If mankind prayed for each other, the

intruder would never enter your home. That is the lesson."

Not wanting to listen any more, I said quietly, "I'd kill him."

"I know," the Archangel acknowledged sadly. "But do you think that is what God wants?"

A quietness descended over us. I tried to explain self-defense, survival.

"I understand," he said, his voice deep with emotion. "But that is not my question."

"I don't care to answer your question."

"Because you know the answer in your heart."

Clenching my fists, I yelled, "Don't tell me any more! You have definitely picked the wrong person. You should have picked some peace-loving New Ager, or even a monk. Somebody who lights incense, chants and believes angels visit regular people. I read Barrons and practice a martial art. I believe angels came only to Biblical figures—a long time ago. I'll never be able to live the way you want me to." I paused, "And I'll *never* be able to tell anyone this."

He nodded again, as if he already knew my path—but didn't share it with me. "Let's talk of other things," he said.

"Please." I was more than willing to get off that subject.

"Intuition," he said.

"What about it?" I asked.

"You, as everyone, has it, but rarely listen to it. Intuition is no more than seeing time at a different level. All time runs concurrently. If intuition appears, you can see the path ahead of you. You should listen, unlock, and accept this gift of your divine soul. There is knowledge there. It is there to help, guide, and protect you.

"You can glimpse the future, if you need to, so take

advantage of that. Time is all the same."

"I don't understand."

Patiently, he replied. "Listen to the intuition within you. It is buried along with the soul. Yet there are messages trying to escape all the time. Some are of prayer, some are of daily habits, some are of profound meaning. Listen to the songs of your soul."

"What other songs are there?"

"There are so many songs," he said, looking toward the sky. "The heavens are filled with melodies. You will see and hear them, as the soul is released from its captivity. Listen to your soul, listen to your intuition. Accept, unlock and most of all, pray.

"For without prayer, without God, nothing is possible. But with Him, all things are possible."

He spoke the words so easily, so richly. All the answers seemed so simple to him. I could not help asking, "Why do we have to struggle like this? Why can't we reach your level?"

He shook his head. "My level is not higher than yours. You have all the knowledge, you just don't know how to tap it. I am here to help you. I am a servant of God. It is a blessing to help you on this journey."

I swallowed hard. He seemed so sincere. Still I was concerned about many things. What if some of these lessons didn't conform to the teachings of the Church? Just the thought of that possibility terrified me. I was not the holiest person, but I certainly didn't want to be excommunicated.

"This all follows what Christ preached. 'Love your neighbor.' Pray. Where does it contradict?"

I didn't know. "Maybe, the intuition lesson?" I said hesitantly.

"It is not mysterious," he said, resting his hands on his lap, and watching the sea waves crash on the shore. "It is a part of you. You can see time and make decisions concerning your life. You have divine guidance with you all the time. Listen to this guidance.

"You have freedom of will, freedom of choice. But listen always to your choices. This is where many of you fail. You listen only to the world, only to yourselves. And worry about your own protection. If you listened to the divinity, listened to God's voice, your answers would be defined, your questions would disappear. Everything would appear clear to you. Your path would be so simple."

He continued, turning to look down at me. His presence, although large, was glowing and comforting. "Pray. Pray to God and pray for each other. In this time of evil and fear, prayer is of the utmost importance. It can stop all hatred. It is a powerful tool on earth and in the heavens. It is within you all the time, this essential tool of life, and many of you have forgotten that it is there. You have forgotten that prayer is the only tool you need.

"Accept. Unlock. And Pray."

I sighed. It was a lot to comprehend. "Do you know that I haven't even reread these transcripts? I'm terrified that I'm making everything up...that I am losing my mind."

"No. You are not," he said. "Is this not for the greater good?"

I barely nodded. I knew his words sounded like scripture, but I still had real doubts. Doubts about him and applying the messages. The only message that sounded easy was listening to my intuition.

He smiled again. "That is not the easiest. The world

crowds you with its problems, its signals, its messages. The intuition which lives within you, God speaking to you, becomes barely a whisper. Animals live more by intuition than humans. They listen to God's plan for them, and wisely follow it.

"Pray to retrieve the lost spiritual gifts which abide within. Pray to retrieve them, to accept them, and continue on your divine path. This is a time of difficulty for everyone. But God is there, although many struggle to find Him. He is always with you, as are His messengers. God never leaves, only you leave.

"Reach deep within yourselves and unlock your spirit."

My voice cracked. "You'll pray for me? Because this is too difficult a challenge alone." And I added—as if he hadn't heard it enough—that he had picked the wrong person for these messages.

He smiled. "I picked the one who needs it the most."

"Go to Bosnia," I said, half flippantly, thinking of all the atrocities which had happened there.

"We have," he answered somberly. "But you must pray for them. Pray for all of them."

I could not process any more. "Could we stop for a while?"

He nodded, then disappeared. The sky above the beach was cloudless. The sun still shone; the air had turned cold and crisp. I wrapped my sweater around my body, although I was not chilled. Inhaling the air, it tasted like nothing I have ever breathed. It was fresher and cleaner than I could possibly describe.

The Archangel was gone, but the air itself seemed like his gift to me.

An hour later, as rain pelted against the window, I realized my "session" with the Archangel was not quite over. Very frequently, immediately after an episode, I felt the Archangel—or the knowledge—still trying to communicate with me.

Sometimes, I acknowledged it and other times I was too exhausted. This day, I switched off my computer and listened.

Although I did not visualize the Archangel, I heard him, not as a voice booming from above, but an inner voice—strong and unique in its purpose. He continued to speak about "loving your neighbor."

"I already know that," I said.

"Ah," he said, in mock surprise. "We did not realize that you had already accepted the lesson and fulfilled it. We do not continue to teach, if the lesson has already been learned." He paused, and added quizzically, "You harbor only love and goodness for everyone?"

"No," I answered, miffed at his sense of humor. "But, I've heard you repeat this 'love your neighbor' many times. I've got the idea. I'd like to move on to something else."

"We can move on," he said, "but your progress will always be impeded. How can one graduate from one level to another without absorbing the lessons? The graduations become meaningless. Such is this, with your lesson of love."

"My lesson?"

"All of your lessons," he said. "Some of you realize this, and can accept, and thus, give love much easier. If you accept the divinity within yourselves, accept God's love all the time and open yourself to these gifts of grace, then you will be

able to love. It will come naturally."

He concluded, "All of this is possible through prayer."

Six

Comfort

Each morning the call beckoned me. I tried to ignore it. Strange as it may sound, I did not want to continue my meetings with the Archangel. Although his presence itself was no longer frightening, the messages still confounded me and I feared my sanity might slip away.

As I closed my eyes, tucked my feet beneath my knees and regulated my breath, I blocked out the distractions around me. I heard a murder of crows cawing in the background, but they became a distant sound as my mind followed its familiar route to London. I found myself descending more stairs into a massive, circular library. Blocks and blocks of books surrounded me. The stacks rose ceiling high, and a crystal slab sat in the center of this huge room. Next to the slab, a man waited for me. A gray beard hung from his angular chin; he wore a flowing brown robe, similar to a monk's cassock. He appeared very old in wisdom, but younger in years. "I am the keeper of the books," he said,

introducing himself.

"What are these books?" I asked, touching the rich leather bindings.

"Each book is a person's life."

From where I stood, I saw small angels flying from one book to another, inscribing in each of them.

"They are transcribing the people's lives," the Book Keeper said, nodding toward the cherubs. "They are my helpers."

I moved slowly toward the crystal slab, running my fingers lightly over the stone. I felt, as well as saw, inscriptions carved into the slab, but I could not understand them. Both the alphabet and the language were foreign to me. I wondered how I could feel the inscriptions, yet know the stone was smooth?

"It is the same hard covering which seals your souls," he said, pulling up a small wooden stool. He sat down and continued to talk. "Once you have broken through the material, then you will be able to read and understand this clearly. It is there for the taking."

"This makes no sense."

"Your soul has all the answers. Divinity has all the answers," he explained patiently, folding his smooth hands onto his lap. "Your soul must be nourished. It is the life-giving force of your body. The minute one cell divides into another at conception, the spirit has arrived. Life has begun. You must be very careful not to separate the spirit from the body, or else death will result."

"What do you mean?" I asked. I had no intentions of leaving my body.

"This message is not for you," the Book Keeper said

clearly. "It is for another. Do not separate the spirit from the body, or death will result. The journey on earth is to combine the two. Let the spirit guide the body, then allow the body to help nourish the spirit. Through love. This will help the spirit grow on another level. It will help you to mature spiritually."

I breathed in deeply, as if trying to control something in my life, and pressed my hands together to keep them from shaking.

"It is your body fighting the message of the soul," the Book Keeper said. "You find it easier to work solely within the body, disregarding the soul. But it is not. The soul becomes so buried, no one realizes that it is the life-giving organ. Not the heart or the lungs. The doctors do not realize this, but without the soul there is no life." He paused, barely moving from his stool, "To live longer and happier in your bodies, you must nourish and feed your souls."

By this point, I felt tired. As I looked at the Book Keeper, I wondered if my imagination had conjured him up. If so, what a horrible person I must be. What if this were evil?

He sensed my question. "Is it for the greatest good?"

I didn't answer immediately. Reviewing the messages, they all seemed for the good—nourish the soul, pray. Yet I wondered aloud, "Why have you brought me to these books?"

"You are only a vehicle," he answered. "But through this you will learn some of the lessons. You will begin to pray for your enemies." His voice seemed to echo through the room. He added, "The world will learn this lesson, but it will take centuries."

"Centuries?" I said. "I don't have centuries."

"Yes, you do," he said emphatically. He rose from the stool, and buried his arms and hands beneath the robes. "The soul is eternal, it will continue on without your body. It will continue growing and loving. Eventually, it will rest with the eternal love of Christ. There it will be fulfilled, it will be one with Christ. The pathway, although it should be simple, becomes difficult for humanity. All the answers and questions are within you—you must listen to your soul. If humanity would only listen to itself, its pathway would accelerate. Humanity puts up constant barriers, blocking out the messages of the souls. It tries to discover a quicker, easier route to happiness. The soul has all the answers, all the happiness. It will guide you toward God."

I argued, "It isn't simple. If it were, miracles would be everyday occurrences."

"They are," he said evenly.

"Like what?" I winced at the tone of my own question. It sounded as if I had a chip on my shoulder, as if I were saying, 'Prove it. Show me.' Yet, I did not stop. "Where were all the angels and messengers when Tom's young friend died of brain cancer a few weeks ago?"

"They were surrounding him," the Book Keeper said, with a wave of his arm.

Looking to where he had pointed, I saw the cherubs writing in the books.

"Do not assume they are only here," the Book Keeper said. "They are always with the dying. Helping them to make the journey, singing to them, guiding them to the light. It is not a fearful experience." We watched as a small angel rubbed his hands over the pages of a book. "And miracles," the man added, "occur every day."

He reached for a book, opened it, and handed it to me.

I clutched the book and looked at the yellowed page. Inside, I saw my car at a nearby intersection. It was evident from the scene that someone had run a red light, slamming into my passenger side. My car had been pushed into an oncoming car. Ambulances and policemen were everywhere. Not only was my car demolished, but I saw myself—all too clearly—being taken away on a stretcher. Just from the looks on the faces of the paramedics, I could tell my prognosis was not good.

"What was that?" I asked, my heart racing faster than ever.

"That was a miracle," he said simply. "You pray, and miracles occur and you never even know about them. The drunk driver missed your car by seconds. That accident never happened. It was not yet your time, but it could have been. A miracle interceded for you. Pray, and when it is for the good, miracles occur."

I dug my fingernails into the binding of the book, and weakly mumbled, "Thank you."

"Do not thank me," he said. "Thank God and continue to pray. Tell everyone that miracles occur all around them, all the time, and they are oblivious to them. They think only miracles they witness are true. There are thousands upon thousands of unseen, and therefore, unrecognized, miracles.

"Thank God for all the goodness which does protect you. Continue to pray for the return of souls, continue to pray for your enemies. Remember that all things are possible. Time is of the essence. We know that the world is a dangerous place. People have forgotten their wisdom, they are concerned with the moment, concerned with their bodily

survival. Greed and lust are temptresses."

The Book Keeper glided slowly across the room, placing his hand on my shoulder. His eyes were tender and filled with kindness. "Go now and pray for one another. Help one another's souls. Each person's soul is yours. You are one with each other. One with God. By praying for each other, you will be helped, your prayers will be answered. Love one another. Love yourself.

"God is always with you," he continued, not moving his hand. "Listen to His call. Listen to His messages."

"I must leave," I said, knowing that he understood my misgivings. With all this beauty and knowledge surrounding me, why didn't I feel perfect contentment?

"You have not yet seen paradise," he said. "Your journey is to overcome the barriers, to listen to the call. You make it difficult, when it is not. But someday, I assure you, you will accept and feel the peace which surrounds you." From within the folds of his robe, he took out a diamond. He handed it to me, "The Archangel left this for you. If I believed you were ready to accept it."

"What is it?" I asked, recognizing another of the gifts.

"Comfort. The Comfort of God is everywhere. Hold it closely. It will warm and help you. Let God comfort you."

I wrapped my fingers tightly around the stone, feeling a surge of warmth flow through my hand.

The Book Keeper tucked his hands deep within his garment, and said softly, "We will continue to pray for you."

"Thank you," I said humbly. "May I go now?"

"Of course," he said, moving away from me. His robe swept the wooden floor beneath him. "You have much to think about. And much to do. Foremost, listen to the songs

of your soul."

As before, although the "session" was over and I had finished transcribing, I felt like a magnet drawn toward metal. Still at my computer, I closed my eyes briefly and asked a question which had been nagging at me. "Why don't you just appear to the people who are in the darkness?"

The Archangel answered me. He was standing in the Book Keeper's library, towering over the stacks and the smaller cherubs. The Book Keeper was nowhere in sight. "Most of you are in darkness," the Archangel said. "But, those who are truly in the darkness cannot hear our call. They need the intercession of another to be saved. Therefore, we must come to their brothers and sisters. You are your brother's keeper."

"That's simple for you to say," I said quietly. I tried to explain the difficulties of just surviving...keeping yourself going...praying for family and friends.

He ignored my protests. "The prayers for your enemies are the strongest prayers the heavens hear. They are truly unselfish. The unselfish prayers are always strong and vivid, and are listened to quickly."

I retorted: "I think that maybe you should listen more intently to the prayers for babies, innocent people, people who are sick with AIDS or cancer before you go answering prayers for evil people. For criminals in jail for murder and rape."

He replied solemnly, "Who prays for them? They are the forgotten. They have souls filled with delight and divinity, also. But they have turned from God for one reason or another, and they cannot find their way back again. It is

essential that their brothers pray for them."

"I would rather keep good people in my prayers."

"That is not your decision," he said quite adamantly.

Swallowing hard, my throat tightened. The anxiety which I had felt before, again returned. I stared at him intently, as if trying to capture his faith.

"Hold onto your gifts," the Archangel said. "You have Grace, Patience, and Comfort. Embrace them. God is with you, all the time. Open the doors and listen to the songs.

"Pray for those who are in desperate need of the prayers. Pray for the souls in darkness, pray for the salvation of the world. The Word will become incarnate, and you will be blessed. As will everyone. All of these prayers will go for goodness. Souls will be saved and returned to God. When this occurs, the love will return to you. Everything selfless results in growth of the soul. It is imperative that you listen to this message. Heed the words."

"It's much easier to listen," I said, "than to heed."

"You are very difficult," the Archangel said, yet he did not appear annoyed.

"Why did you pick me?" I asked. Although I still was not comfortable with these visits, the thought of an Archangel instructing me, gave me a sense individuality. A sense of worth.

"Because you are common," he answered flatly.

"Oh," I said.

"No," he said, shaking his head, "it is not an insult. You have the doubts of man, you have the questions of man, but you are also concerned with Goodness and doing right. Even so, you have not always listened to the messages which have been sent to you. You are like the others, indicative of the

others. You have the same fears, the same concerns." He paused, as if letting out a breath, and concluded, "You are representative."

"Anything else?" I asked, very miffed that I wasn't 'special.'

The Archangel continued, deflating my ego. "You are all one. When love is everywhere, which eventually will occur through prayer, everything will change. Heaven will be on Earth. You will be astounded at the miracles which surround you. Spirits will soar with Divinity and lightness. But, this journey must begin with each individual soul. You must start by praying for each other. You *must* be your brother's keeper.

"Your heart does not want to crack its armor, does not want to display the soul. This does not come easily for you, but miracles will become daily occurrences. The spirit has undying energy and it will grow and consume you for the good. Let it begin with each of you. Pray and listen to the Word. Listen to the ways of God. Help one another.

"I cannot stress how important Prayer is."

As the Archangel spoke, I felt exhaustion run through my body. I asked, "Could we continue this later?"

He smiled, his face awash with a brilliant, white light. "Certainly. We have waited centuries, one more day will not deter us. Continue to pray, as we pray for you."

"Besides you, other angels pray for me?"

"Of course," he said, towering over me. "Our prayers have helped you listen to this call. We are all around you, waiting to guide you toward the light. Toward the Word of God. It begins with you, and if you are willing to accept the gifts which surround you, it will be an easy and pleasurable journey." His eyes, large and blue, were filled with an

immeasurable kindness. "The more you do for your brethren, the more you do for Christ. Each act results in a greater love, and your spirit will be filled with God."

His words were so beautiful, I tried to let them sink in.

After what seemed like a few minutes of silence, I asked him if he needed to tell me anything else that day. I explained that I had a lot of research to do on my thesis.

"You have God's work to do," he said matter-of-factly. "There is no other work."

"Oh, yes there is," I said, thinking about my deadlines.

"Listen to us," he said. "There is no other work, but the work of the Spirit. Everything else in life will be easily accomplished, because you have put your priorities with God and the Spirit. The largest task is listening to the Soul, listening to the Divinity, hearing the Spirit, and becoming one with the Word."

My head ached thinking of it all.

"That is enough for today," he said, dismissing me with a gentle wave of his hand. "Go and rest. Think about the messages we have told you. They are many, but there are more to come. Call upon God, call upon the angels, accept the gifts. They are endless and always ready.

"Everything is for your growth. Everything we speak of is for your salvation, your soul. Draw in the breath of the Holy Spirit, and allow Him to fill your lungs with His life. Slowly, the armor will begin to fall away, as you pray for your brothers."

I rubbed my temple. "You must pray very hard for me. I'm not a bad person, but you're asking me to accomplish a difficult task."

He nodded. "Now you understand one of your lessons.

For others, there are different lessons, but for all, they result in Love God and Love your neighbor. And pray for the Word."

Seven

"They Are Not My Concern"

The following day, I didn't have time to sit, pray, and transcribe. Besides which, something told me I would not like the message. So, I tried to ignore it. Tom and I were traveling to South Korea in a few days, and I had lots of last-minute errands. We were looking forward to practicing Tae Kwon Do at the Korean University, but the daily news of a nuclear standoff with North Korea troubled me. As I packed our things, I wondered if we were making the right decision.

In the midst of packing, I stopped. I felt a silent beckoning to my soul. Abandoning my half-filled suitcase, I sat down. Within seconds, I had taken the familiar route to the beach. The Archangel waited for me on the sands, but it was obvious we were not staying. With a gentle touch of his hand, he motioned me to follow him.

Immediately, I realized my intuition had been right. I did not want to be at this destination. We were in a small

inner-city apartment, witnessing a horrible scene. A young couple were having sex on a dirty mattress in a corner, as a third woman sat at a kitchen table snorting heroin. In the corner, small babies cried in a filthy crib. The adults paid no attention to the children.

"Take me back," I pleaded, grabbing the Archangel's arm.

"Look at these people," he said.

I turned my head away. "They are not my concern."

"Yes, they are," he replied firmly.

"Listen," I said, just as firmly—angrily in fact, "you don't understand. I try to lead a decent life. These people should, too. It would be easy to take drugs, break the law. But, I don't. These people," I said, pointing toward the squalid scene, "disgust me. They should take responsibility for their lives."

The Archangel didn't answer me. Quietly, he brought me to the room across the corridor. A young woman lay unconscious on a bed, with a needle sticking out of her arm. Her face was beaten, and covered with blood. Cockroaches scurried on the kitchen counter, amidst rancid meat. Before I could protest, he took me to a house in Georgia, then a trailer in New Hampshire. All of the scenes were sad, violent, or revolting.

Finally we arrived in a room where a father was sexually abusing a small child. I spun around. Screaming at the Archangel, I yelled, "Why are you subjecting me to this? I can't do anything about it. If I start going into the inner cities, I'll be murdered."

"I did not ask you to do what you cannot," he said, looking intently at me. "That is not what I have been asked

to tell you. I have been asked to show you this." He turned his head toward the terrible scene.

Looking at the father, fat and sweaty, his hand covering the poor child's mouth, I felt angry and disgusted. "See that guy?" I said, pointing toward the father. "You keep telling me to pray for my enemies, for their salvation. But, *you* don't get it." I paused to catch my breath. "He's a horrible, evil man!" Turning my back on the scene, I continued to berate the Archangel. "I don't care if that man finds salvation," I said. "As a matter of fact, he should burn in Hell for eternity."

"You are all one," the Archangel replied.

"Stop it!" I cried, pressing my hands against my ears. "I am *not* one with him. I don't care if he is saved."

The Archangel's voice was unfaltering. "Until the last of you is saved, none will be."

Until the last of you is saved, none will be. I stopped dead. That was not what I had learned. "We're here to save our own souls," I said.

"Love your enemies, pray for your enemies," he continued. "While you harbor any ill will, you will not reach God. That is the key, so you might as well begin now. Start by praying for their salvation. Your salvation will result."

Needing to clarify his words, I stammered. "I must've misheard you. I don't want my salvation to be dependent on other people finding God."

"You must pray for everyone," he said. "Then that prayer will be returned to you. Once all hatred is gone, love and God will live within all. God does not want anyone to turn toward the darkness."

None of this settled well with me. The whole message, the glimpses into other people's worlds...I was terribly

confused. Yet, I repeated, I did not want to pray for people who should be helping themselves. "Why don't you knock on their doors? Tell them these messages, not me."

The Archangel clasped his hands together, as if praying. "They cannot hear me," he said sadly, "without your intercession. Without your prayers. The prayers of the world are essential for God to reach those in darkness. You have a responsibility."

"I don't want it," I answered defiantly.

"That is your choice. But eventually, at some time, you will accept it. As will everyone. You must all pray for each other. These prayers will be answered.

"None of you realize the strength of the prayers. God is all knowing and all powerful. Prayers are the most powerful tool available—stronger than nuclear bombs, stronger than any of your weapons, or armors, or medicines. Lives can be changed, saved, and altered through these prayers. The more often people pray, the stronger the call becomes collectively. Miracles will occur every moment, souls will be saved." He concluded, "That is the message."

That was ample, I thought. The places we had seen were frightening, yet thinking I was responsible for others' salvation terrified me even more. It seemed unjust.

Picturing the scenes again, I remembered the small child. Prayers for the child came easily to me, but no matter how hard I tried, I could not pray for her father. It made no sense; he was evil.

Even as I wondered if the Archangel's message was right, I found myself defending it. I heard the words, "Do not judge. It is not for you to do that, but only to pray for their salvation. Love your neighbor as yourself."

Eight

Prayer Versus War Games

Early April

Tom and I had traveled to both South Korea and Florida within two weeks. Following the advice of seasoned travelers, I didn't drink any alcoholic beverages on the 18 hour flight to Seoul. Yet, as the plane hit turbulence, I wished I had ordered something stronger than mineral water. As the 727 dipped slightly, my fingers clutched the seat. I called upon the Archangel. Immediately, he was there—in my mind—comforting me. North Korea's threats of nuclear war vanished from my mind. Even as the plane lurched, the Archangel's presence brought me a serenity and a calm which I had never before experienced.

Again, I wondered, what was occurring?

As we toured South Korea, walked through the Kirim-sa Temple and heard the Buddhist monks chant, I realized that the Archangel's words were taking root within me. In the midst of a different culture, thousands of miles from home,

the words "you are all one" repeated themselves in my mind.

My intentions were good, but my spiritual thoughts were fleeting. At our Tae Kwon Do lessons at the Korean University, I ferociously kicked, yelled, and punched my opponents. Although I had listened to the Archangel's messages, I was not ready to live them, nor "pray" for my attacker.

Once we arrived back in Connecticut, I heard the call again. This time, as opposed to earlier visits, I felt relaxed—not anxious. After a two week absence from the messages, I *wanted* to meet with the Archangel.

As I prayed, I entered the bookstore. It was almost empty. Intuitively, I sensed that whatever knowledge had been there, I had learned. Descending more stairs, I arrived at the library. It was still filled with books. Since no one waited there, I called for the Archangel. Immediately, I was propelled to the beach, and a beautiful woman, with flowing robes, descended from the crystal-blue sky. A crate filled with diamonds, more gifts, appeared next to her. Surrounding her shoulders were clusters of small angels, hovering by her side. The angels were the size of toddlers; their expressions were filled with innocence. I was silent as the Heavenly Woman approached me and conveyed a stream of knowledge.

"Humanity is born with everything it needs to know, but the lesson is to APPLY it," she said softly. "It is the most difficult lesson there is because we try to forget this knowledge. Without knowledge, we are not accountable. Therefore, excuses can be made, 'I did not know, therefore, how was I suppose to act?'"

Her manner was calming; her voice a gentle whisper.

"Each of us is born with divinity. Babies are born, mostly composed of spirit, with hardly any body. They know all the answers, know all the applications. They love completely, but as they grow, they bury the knowledge. They become involved with the concerns of the people surrounding them. The divine is buried more and more as we grow older. The body and its demands take over."

She paused, "All of which is a perfect excuse not to 'APPLY.'"

"I realize I should love," I said, "But it's much easier said than done. How can I do it?"

The angels fell silent. The Heavenly Woman looked at me tenderly. Happiness and peace seemed to penetrate the air. "I will pray for you. Every time you have difficulty loving someone, you must pray. Not for yourself, but for them. It is a more difficult task to pray for others, especially those whom you find difficult to love."

I quibbled with her, told her about evil people, but she continued patiently. "You do not have to surround yourself with these people. Positive energy results in positive energy. But you must not ignore them, you must pray for them. In essence, this goodness will come back to you."

The diamonds shone brilliantly, and the angels floated silently next to her. The beach seemed like a heavenly place, but I was not peaceful. "Why not?" I asked.

The Heavenly Woman smiled again. "Because you realize that you are receiving a responsibility. You must act on our advice; you can no longer pretend you did not receive it. The Bible has told people for centuries how to live; some have ignored it, some have forgotten it, some pretend they don't see it. But it is there. These messages, too, are a

responsibility. You cannot, try as you might, ignore them. We have been calling to your spirit for years, but you have said it is frightening, perhaps evil. Evil has even tried to keep you away from this blessing."

I listened.

"All of you carry this message," she continued. "This message within you."

"How do I know if it's right?" I asked.

"It is for good. It is for the greater good," she said, as she made the sign of the cross. "Write it down and remember it. Apply the lessons which you hold in your heart. All knowledge is there, all goodness is there. It has been buried because remembering it will bring responsibilities. You will be changed for the better. You will feel the need to pray for others. You will have to relinquish the hate, the envy, the revenge which grows in your heart each day that the divinity is buried."

Reflecting on her words, I felt tired and lonely. I realized she was right: I didn't want to know these lessons, because I might have to live them. Praying for myself and for my family was difficult enough, never mind praying for my enemies.

"What about the terrible injustices in life?" I asked. "Take the poor crack cocaine babies...how can anyone pray for their mothers?"

Her manner stayed even, never condemning or dismissive of me, even when I argued. "It is wrong for someone to bury the spirit of the baby. The crack addict has pushed her own darkness onto her child, and in doing so, has helped bury the child's spirit. This child is not born with the freedom of spirit; it is already burdened with the

problems of the flesh."

"Abortion?"

The Heavenly Woman reached for my hand and softly caressed it. "It is not for one to deny another their journey. Each soul needs the opportunity to fulfill their lessons, to apply their knowledge to this world."

Questions begin tumbling out of me. "This world?" The way she had phrased it, I wondered if we had been here before.

She smiled again, obviously pleased with my thirst for knowledge. "That is not of concern. The concern is how you apply your divinity in this world. I assure you that there is a Heaven and Hell. The lesson is to apply what you already know. It is simple to know, difficult to practice. APPLY, apply your divinity. Tap into your soul. Pray, pray, pray. For others and the world."

Her words, spoken so firmly, so truthfully, echoed on the deserted beach. "Prayer is the strongest signal," the Heavenly Woman continued, "It is impenetrable. And God will always answer."

"I wish I felt a total peace and comfort in these words," I said. Only when I looked at her did my soul glimpse serenity.

"Look into my face," she said, reading my thoughts. Still caressing my hand, her skin smooth and lovely, she added. "I will be with you. This is not a comfortable road for you. This is a birth, and it is never easy. It is easier to turn away, stay in the womb, warm and dark. But that is not what you were meant to do. Nor was anyone."

"But why me?"

She smiled. "It is not just you, you are not special. I stress

that. Everyone has this divinity, has these messages within them. They have the knowledge of God. They are God's children; they are divine. Their spirit is like His. And within your bodies, all of this rests as if wrapped in gold, though lost down in the basement of your bodies. You must search for this gift, this package. Be careful not to store it in some place of honor. Open it up, unwrap it, and use it. It is the salvation of the world. It is God within you. It is His message, His love, His hope for the world.

"Everyone has this gift, everyone. Pray for each other. Pray for the world. And open your gifts. We call to everyone. Some are so burdened by life's problems—the sin, the materialism, the guilt—that they never hear the angels beckoning. But, the angels beckon to all.

"You must sit still in the divinity and open yourself up. In doing so, you are opening the golden gift within you. It has always been there, from God to you. It is for you to open, not partially, but fully. And to Use. You must use it."

I kept my hand in hers, taking comfort in her grasp.

"Once the gift is opened, the call is even louder. The responsibility is there. You must listen to the call. You have been hearing us for years, and your fear and Evil have kept you away. Fear is darkness, and the Devil does not want you to listen to this message. But, it is for the good of your soul, for the good of the world.

"Finally, you heard the calling of your soul. Now, take the package and open it, and you will experience beauty, light, and a peace which only comes from God.

"You must apply this divinity in your life."

"Don't you understand?" I asked, my voice cracking. "I don't know how to pray for my enemies." Tears of frustration

fell down my cheeks.

"The more you pray, the more it will become like breathing."

I swallowed hard. "What if I become a religious fanatic? Obsessed? Talking to spiritual figures, listening to messages?" I swallowed again, my voice barely audible, "What if I lose my sanity?"

"I am with you, as are these angels," she said, raising her hands to acknowledge the small winged creatures around her. "God is with you. Your lesson is to pray for others and that prayer will return to you."

Her face radiated maternal love.

As we sat on the rock, I cast down my eyes, ashamed at my thoughts. Summoning up the courage, I explained that in Florida we had played a game called, "War Games." Each participant received a gun, filled with paint pellets, and the objective was to "kill" the enemy team. Initially, I had no interest in playing, but was finally coerced into it. "It will be fun," the group said. "It's just a game. Like hide and seek, but with paint guns." As the game progressed over the hot afternoon, I hid beneath bushes, stalking my victims. I was consumed with survival—eager to shoot and hunt down the enemy. It had become more than just a game. I enjoyed it.

"What kind of person am I?"

Evenly, she replied, "We sent you to that game."

My mouth dropped open. "Sent me?"

"Yes," she said. The sun was low over the ocean, and a gentle breeze blew across our faces as the Heavenly Woman spoke. "It is important for you to remain humble. It is hard for people to realize how evilness works. They think it happens to someone else, but it is everywhere. It is only

through the grace of God that you are saved."

"What about our own accomplishments? Praying for each other's salvation?"

She nodded. "They are important in that they turn you toward God, and God in his goodness bestows grace on you. The more worthy actions you perform, the closer you become to God's grace. And thus, salvation."

She told me that I had criticized the Serbs in Bosnia for their atrocities, but that I, too, was as capable of performing such heinous acts.

I cringed at her words. "In real life?" I asked, thinking of my zest to "kill" my opponent in the War Games. "Am I capable of such hatred?"

"You are all one," the Heavenly Woman answered. "Whatever your brother does, you have done. Therefore, it is essential that you all turn toward God for the salvation of yourselves and the earth.

"And Evil is very prevalent. You must pray for each other. And your enemies."

The breeze intensified. As I looked at the Heavenly Woman, I noticed that the wind did not disturb her clothing. Everything around her was still. Smiling, she said, "I am pleased with you."

"Pleased?" I blurted.

"Yes," she said. "After you played the War Game, you reflected on your actions. You listened to your soul. It is a long journey for you, and you have made much improvement."

"But, I *liked* the game."

She shook her head. "You realized that you were capable—even in a simulated game of hate and anger—of

horrendous actions. The same actions for which you have harshly judged others. It is for you to pray for one another, not judge one another."

Amidst a chorus from the angels, the Heavenly Woman ascended into the sky. "With prayer, all things are possible."

Watching the sea waves break, I sat alone on the rock, absorbing the words which had been spoken to me. Soon afterward, the Archangel appeared at my side. He seemed larger than ever, as he settled next to me. The wings rustling behind him were huge, golden and white, with a slight transparency. I smiled at him.

"We are always with you," he said. "You realize that."

"Will I always be able to speak with you?"

He shook his head. "You will not always be able to see us, or access us, as you do now. You have this opportunity for a short time. Until our message is clear, until your journey with this message is completed."

"I don't understand."

"You will," he promised me.

"During the next few days," the Archangel continued, "others will bear messages. Let the messages be known."

"Uh oh," I said, hearing the apprehension in my voice. "What do you mean, 'let the messages be known?' People won't believe me. They'll lock me up."

"Do not be concerned," he said. "People are in need of the messages. They are waiting for them. You may be ridiculed, but it will be inconsequential."

Clenching my teeth, the beautiful beach no longer seemed so peaceful. Even the crashing of the waves disturbed me. My heart was palpitating again as I argued with him.

"Your plans are not necessarily God's," he replied firmly. "Call upon us. More messages will begin tomorrow." With that, he disappeared into the clouds.

After the meeting, as I transcribed the conversations, I wondered once again if I were making all this up. After all, I had written fiction before; what made this so different?

Then, quite clearly, as I sat at the computer, I heard the words again. "All of this is for the good. The message is something the world needs. Souls know they are one with each other, but have forgotten this knowledge. They need to be reminded of their purposes on Earth. They need to be told that everyone is One, they are one Soul, one Divinity, one child of God's. All must turn toward God for their salvation."

The Voice continued as I typed. "It is a difficult premise, having to save every last one in order to save all. But, that is the lesson of love. What is love without sacrificing? Without helping each other? Without judging? Each must learn the lesson, and those who have learned it, must teach it. Until all is love. Until all are one with God, united in the Spirit.

"It is time for the message to be revealed," the Voice continued. "You know that this is not your voice, because you are writing faster than you can think. This is the Voice of help and spirit. Please tell the others to Pray and look inside themselves. There they will find peace, they will find strength, they will find grace and love. And foremost, they will find God.

"Once they access this divinity, all the horrors of the world will disappear, because the two cannot survive together. And the divinity of the soul is much stronger. Each

of you will be drawn towards this light, once it has entered your life. But it is only with prayer and the help of the others that some will search for the light."

My fingers flew over the keys. "The darkness can be comfortable and tempting. But it is immediately crushed by the light. Please listen to this Word, please pray for each other. Especially for those whom you care for the least. It will help both of you. You are saved through your sisters and brothers."

After transcribing the Voice's dictation, I wondered why it no longer frightened me.

Nine

Honor

Before the next meditation began, I already knew its topic. While driving the day before, the word "Honor" was revealed. I realized intuitively that three visits would occur, and prior to the first, I was to ponder the word "Honor."

As I settled down to pray, my mind traveled the same path, but instead of descending a staircase, I entered a tunnel of rushing blue water, none of which touched me. I was protected from the onslaught of water. Emerging from this water tunnel, I walked into a field of daffodils. Bees buzzed lightly from flower to flower.

A small, bubbling cherub, greeted me. Surrounding him was an aura of yellow light. "Honor," he said.

I attempted to smile, but the heat stifled me and I feared bee stings. The beauty of the place did not impress me. The Cherub must have read my mind, because suddenly a cool breeze wafted across the field. Despite this, I still felt

uncomfortable. The Cherub smiled and laughed, and immediately took me to the beach.

"You are the most accepting here," he said. Then he added, "I gave you the word 'Honor' yesterday, because I could not wait." His small heart-shaped face was filled with delight as he flitted around me. At times, he settled briefly on the rock, only to fly off again. His wings were a milky-white transparency, and his small body was clothed in silver material, with iridescent threads. He seemed very different, in both appearance and personality, than the other messengers. I told him my observation, and he beamed.

"I am new," he said, his face radiating joy. "We all have our own personalities. Just because we have lessons to teach and love to learn, it does not mean we are identical." His body was buoyant and joyous. He reminded me of a butterfly, skipping from one place to another, excited with his mission.

"Honor the divinity within each other," he said. "This is the first of these messages. It is so simple. All of your paths are so simple, but you struggle constantly. Instead of flowing with the river, you fight it. It becomes tiresome and overwhelming and sooo...so...difficult," he dragged the words to emphasize them. "Go with the energy, leave your anxiety aside. Enjoy each moment of this wonderful gift God has given you."

His voice sounded sweet and melodic. "You must honor each other and yourselves."

I protested. "Some people aren't worthy of honoring."

"The divinity within them is worthy of honor," he said, his voice light. The Cherub seemed to dance above me. "Once humanity realizes that God resides within it, it will

accept and acknowledge His presence in each other. Its pathway will change." He went on to say that many people, especially youths in crime-ridden areas, were committing crimes because they did not truly honor themselves or each other. "If they truly respected themselves, and knew what wonders lay within, they would never abuse their bodies, nor the bodies of others. Self-esteem is part of honor."

He caught his breath, and continued. "Many lack self-esteem. Their lives and their bodies mean nothing to them. They do not see the pathway for this life, because they feel unworthy." The Cherub's voice deepened as he added, "It is everyone's responsibility to give honor to each other. Once honor is accepted as being as important as the bread of the body, lives will begin to change."

"I don't want to honor a murderer," I stated flatly.

The Cherub told me that I was not to honor or condone the action of the murderer. But, honor his soul. By, doing this, the murderer will begin to realize that there is within him a God who loves him. Who can bring him to Salvation.

"Without honoring each other, there is no respect, and love cannot follow." He paused, resting on the rock. The sun was setting over the ocean, yet the air remained warm and humid. The Cherub turned to me. "We have tried to tell you this numerous times, but it is *your* concern, if your neighbor is not living the word according to God. It is *your* responsibility to help one another, to respect and Honor each other."

Although he still smiled, his words were not lightly spoken. "You are not alone on this journey," he said. "Everyone is one."

I hated hearing that again. It was hard enough being

accountable for my own actions, never mind other people's.

"Your actions result in the actions of others," the Cherub said. He flew away from the rock, his face filled with excitement and wondrous joy. "It is so simple," he said, delighting in every word. "If only everyone would wake up from this sleep, and see the ease with which this can be accomplished. When you honor each other, everything will fall into place. Crimes will end, Love will grow, each of you will turn toward God. And thus, He will bestow more Graces upon you.

"We stress that love and acceptance are the most important missions of your lives. We have given you gifts to access the divinity within each other. They are abundant. Now, we are making it even more simple—take this first word: Honor. Honor each other."

I knew about Honor. The Bible teaches us to honor our parents. "But honor in the United States is not something," I told the Cherub, "that we value. We're a democracy here, everyone is equal. We don't even 'honor' the president."

"That is right," he said, nodding excitedly. "Everyone is equal in God's eyes, too. He loves His children mightily. Therefore it is important to honor each other, to seek each other out as peers, as children of God. No matter what the actions, souls are divine. You are accountable for the others."

You are accountable for each other.

The words echoed in my mind. Finally I understood that there were many messages, but Oneness was the essence of them all. And I found it hard to accept. Yet, inside I was changing. A shell was breaking open and something was struggling to emerge. With this birth, I was sure, would come a responsibility... of seeing things differently, of not judging,

of acting kinder. If I followed what the angels were teaching me, everything—good or bad—would return to me.

They had said it was simple. An easy path.

Then why did it all seem so complicated?

Ten

Tolerance and Reverence

Once again, I knew the message before the messenger appeared. As suddenly as a bolt of lightening, the word came into my mind.

Tolerance.

Strange, I thought, dismissing it. Tolerance did not sound holy or enlightened. It sounded just, well, tolerable.

As I sat down to pray, I immediately found myself seated on a tree log. Surrounding me was a deep, lush, green forest; a stream trickled nearby. Before I had a chance to catch my breath, a young woman nodded to me.

She was dressed in a flowing dark green skirt, the same shade of the forest, and a lighter green blouse. Blond hair cascaded over her shoulders as she bent to take my hand.

Even her eyes were a deep, green.

Taking my hand, she caressed it lightly, like a child playing with her mother's fingers. Curious, I crooked my

neck and checked behind her. There were no wings.

"All spirits are available to help you," the Forest Woman said. "I am just another helper."

She told her message: Tolerance and Reverence.

"Tolerance doesn't sound very holy," I said.

"Many will hear the message of Honor," she explained, settling on the bench next to me, "and they will be unable to achieve it without guidance; unable to shift from hatred to love easily. Nor, from hatred to honor. Therefore, I have been sent as an intermediary. To send the message of Tolerance."

With the stream babbling behind us, I strained to hear her soft voice. "Tolerance?" It still didn't make sense.

"It will be the first step for many," she said. "They will move from darkness—hatred—to an almost neutral zone of tolerance. It is not the goal, but it will be necessary for many. This will occur before they fully face Our Lord. From tolerance, they will move to Reverence for God. Then, honor for each other and the Divine."

She told me many things, some of which I cannot recall. After each meeting, I asked the messenger to help me remember. The Forest Woman said, "You will remember what is necessary for the message."

More was told me, but I cannot recall it. Although I recorded the session immediately afterward, all I can visualize of this lost information was the Forest Woman laughing, as I fought against her messages.

"Listening to God's word and living His way is so simple," she explained. Even though this was our first meeting, she knew me well. She had seen me worry over work, school—and stated that it was needless, mental

anguish. She compared such worries to living away from God. "Going to God is so simple. All the energy used in fearing the unknown, makes the journey difficult and hard. It is wasted energy."

She tilted her head toward the distance. "When you cross into His world, and live His Word, you will be amazed at how easy it is. You will be astounded that you did not cross into it immediately."

"Easy?" I asked. "It seems impossible that everyone —including murderers, rapists, child molesters—can all turn toward God."

She shook her head, pushing away a falling strand of hair. The grove in which we sat became cooler, almost chilly, as clouds formed above us. "You are all one," she said, repeating the message I had heard too many times already. "Adam and Eve were not banished from the Garden, you all *turned away* from God. In His goodness, He has let you take the long journey home. In your soul, you crave His presence. You are like homing pigeons, trying to reach your destination. There is interference everywhere, and false signals to confuse you, but eventually, all will band together and return to Him."

"We all sinned?" The notion terrified me.

"You are all one, and when you repent, and return to God, you will return to your true home. Then, you will be astounded at how simple and wonderful is His way. You will be shocked that you had not learned the message more quickly. God's message can only be learned by doing. You must pray—that is a strong action. As the prayers grow stronger for each other, the path to Jesus will broaden and become easy. There will be no more twists and turns, no

more blockages. You will follow the Divine life. All as One. All toward the Spirit."

I felt a warmth cross my face. The clouds had passed, and the afternoon sun—although not hot—felt comforting. "Everything is possible through prayer for each other. Why do you not believe in the power of prayer?" she asked, her voice more audible than before. "After all," she continued, "when you pray, you implore God to listen. Therefore, is not your prayer an extension of His power? All of mankind will be an instrument of His, all of mankind will flourish with prayer for each other."

And then I heard those words again, "You are responsible for each other's salvation."

I did not want to hear this edict.

The Forest Woman grew impatient with me, pursing her lips together. "You are responsible for each other, because you were one and are one. What the left hand does is controlled by the entire body. You cannot separate yourselves.

"Take heart. Breathe deeply. Listen to the Word of God, listen to your heartbeat. In the silence of this, you will begin the journey.

"Many will hear these messages in the next few years. Some will hear them through journals as this, but the words are meant for all. Some will directly experience messages. Others will be prayed for, until they, too, turn toward the divinity which is waiting for them."

"But what about evil?" I asked.

"It is present," the Forest Woman said, folding her hands on her skirt. In the background, birds were singing as if in tune with the stream. "And it is powerful. But with God's

word surrounding you, it cannot survive. Turn toward the spiritual kindness inside all of you. Listen to the calming spirit which resides within you. God has given everyone the defenses which are needed against evil. They are readily accessible. We urge you to listen to them, and use them."

Her hand touched mine, soft and cool, as she handed me a large, old-fashioned key. "Take this," she said, "it will help to unlock some people from hatred and bring them to Tolerance."

Taking the key reluctantly, I told her my misgivings. "Tolerance doesn't sound very profound. Actually," I said, hoping not to be disrespectful, "it sounds rather wishy-washy."

The Forest Woman smiled, as if amused. "You are human. Your path is filled with diversions. Tolerance will bring some, who are badly in need, toward the other messages.

"Tell those who cannot find love, to tolerate."

This woman did not understand how the Earth operated, I thought. I mentioned a serial killer I had seen on the television news.

"You did not pray for him, did you?" she asked.

"No," I said adamantly. "I prayed for the families of his victims. They are the ones wounded and hurt."

"This is fleeting," she said, almost wistfully. The Forest Woman took hold of my hand again. "The victims are already on their spiritual journeys, evolving and growing with God. It is the murderer who is distant from God. It is he who needs your prayers. Remember—you are all One."

"Thank you," I said, raising my hand. "But it all seems impossible. I can't hear anymore."

In a vernacular which surprised me, she told me that I was "as obstinate as they said." Laughing lightly, she patted my hand.

"They?" I asked, startled. "Who are they?"

"Your helpers and messengers for the last thousands of years."

"Thousands of years? I am only 37."

She laughed again. "Sometimes," she agreed, "I believe it."

The Forest Woman continued, "Remember, humanity turned from God at the beginning of creation. It has been working its way home to Him since then. None can be saved until all are saved."

It made no sense. It went against everything I had been taught. For the umpteenth time, I wondered if I were making it all up...if perhaps a fertile imagination had gone over the edge. It would be easier to think that, I surmised, then I wouldn't feel obligated to alter my behavior. Of course, I still didn't have to change my life...but something in these messages rang true. And that was more disturbing.

Eleven

You Have Not Been Listening

During this time, my life continued unchanged...at least the day-to-day activities did. At a fund raiser for the Hartford Ballet, I watched a young, Catholic priest move through the buffet. He worked at an large city parish. 'Here's who I need,' I thought, approaching him. A liberal who welcomes the city's homeless, gays and lesbians to his church...surely he won't discriminate against me.

After briefly discussing the Church, I broached the subject of visions, (not daring to mention my own.) He rolled his eyes, and said, "Oh, *those* people who see apparitions."

Quickly, I returned to the topic of the ballet, relieved not to have divulged my story. Yet, I understood the priest's misgivings—they had been my own. The Bible frequently mentioned angels—in Genesis, the Annunciation, the Nativity, and at Christ's tomb. But these were angels with a mission, appearing to historical, holy figures.

Not to a regular person.

The following day, I prayed. I arrived at the circular library. It was partially empty—cardboard boxes, filled with books and tied with strings, were stacked throughout the aisles. Although I wanted to stay there, I found myself transported to the beach. Standing on the shore, I looked up at the rock on which I usually sat. The climb seemed higher and more dangerous. Out of my reach.

A booming voice startled me from above. It was the Archangel.

"You have not been listening," he bellowed.

I tilted my head upwards and searched for him. He descended from the sky, bathed in a white light, then he stood majestically on the boulder. Although his face still appeared beautiful and kind, his words were angry. Somewhat frightened, I answered, "Of course I've been listening—and writing it down."

"You have not been *living* it," he said.

I gathered my courage. "Writing it down, transcribing it, is much easier than living it," I paused. "You're asking me to accomplish the impossible. Pray for people I don't like, be responsible for everyone..." I cradled my head in my hands, "Don't you understand—even the thought is exhausting?"

"That is the message. Heed it."

As I lifted my head, I watched him rise back into the clouds. His words echoed like a wind through the deserted beach. Within moments, a small angel appeared. She was climbing—not flying—up the large rock. Her body was rounded and chubby, dark curls encircled her head. Even from a distance, I knew she had the same happy personality as the Cherub. I wondered if there were certain similar

characteristics of these small angels.

Then I wondered if I were really going mad.

"Charity," she said, finally arriving at her perch. She reached out a hand to steady herself, and dangled her small legs from the rock.

At her insistence, I climbed up the rock, fearful to look down. Once seated together, I said, "Charity. That's no new message. That's as old as the ages."

The Small Angel's face was young and perky, but her voice had knowledge beyond her physical appearance. "Charity is another method to bring those lost in darkness toward God. Some people must move in steps, slowly. By being charitable, they attain the correct path to hear the Word of God...to be in the right place...to listen to His messages."

"Charity?" I asked. "How do I transcribe that? It seems so...obvious."

"First," she said, firmly, "Tell everyone to *help* their loved ones. Charity involves selflessness, which pleases God. By being selfless, you are in essence helping yourself. You are all One.

"Soon, each person will be charitable to those who are unappreciative. That is the hardest act of all for you."

"For the unappreciative?" I said. "Why bother?"

The Small Angel grinned with childlike excitement. "How many times has God answered the prayers of the people, and how often have they thanked Him? Yet, God continues to grant blessings. His love is unconditional. Through Charity, you, too, will learn to live unconditionally. These are the steps, slow as they may seem, to bring you closer to the Light. Bring you closer to Divinity. Not all can

move easily toward God. Prayer will bring them, but actions must also take place, in order to be receptive to God."

Finally, I had become somewhat comfortable with the presence of the Archangel. But, with these other messengers... I grew worried.

Why was this happening to *me*?

The Small Angel flew from the rock, and flitted across the sands. "What we have told you seem like difficult tasks," she said. "We cannot stress how simple they are, because to you they seem overwhelming. The Bible says all these things, love your neighbor as yourself. Yet, people do not. They do not realize that Your Neighbor Is Yourself.

"You must take these gifts and messages, and use them for Salvation. Pray for each other and the world will be saved. Prayer is the strongest tool. These messages will bring people to a place where they can listen to God's word, a holy place. Prayer will bring them there, but these actions will speed up the process.

"Everything is possible," she continued, her tiny lips forming a perfect smile. "But it is essential to listen to the Word of God."

I inhaled the sea air, trying to control my breathing. Although the Small Angel did not frighten or intimidate me, the messages were still formidable.

"Do not be frightened," she said, reading my thoughts. "The Lord is with you. As are we. We want the World to listen to His Word, to find Love within each other, to be at peace with God. The time is approaching, people are learning and listening to the messages...but they have yet to fully practice them.

"It is essential that you pray and take part in these lessons.

Do not judge your brothers and sisters, no matter what the urge. It is their place to choose their path."

Taking that bit of information in, I asked, "What if some don't ever return to the Light? If we are all One, are we all condemned?"

She shook her head, her eyes widening. "God would never do such a thing. He would not punish you, but He is waiting for all to be saved. That is your mission as a people, and He is patient with you. He is waiting for all His children to return to Him as One.

"Blessed be His Word," she said.

We sat quietly, watching a flock of sea gulls swoop to the surface of the water. Finally, I broke the silence. "I can't find such compassion in my heart," I said sadly. "A friend of mine has an adopted Korean daughter. Recently, a bully at school began taunting the child for racial reasons, even threatening to kill her. How can such pure hatred be in an 8-year-old's soul?" I urged my friend's daughter to defend herself, especially if she were physically attacked. Looking intently at the Small Angel, I added, "You can't understand the fears and pain which accompany a body."

She frowned and folded her hands on her lap. "This is difficult for you," she said. "But you must remember that children have learned their behaviors. Their parents have taught hate. They are not listening to God's Word, and have turned away from His blessings. They must be prayed for, and so must the child."

"Prayer is fine," I said "But for people to change so drastically...we need miracles."

"Miracles are everyday occurrences," she said, her eyes opening wide in surprise. "God's work is always a miracle.

Miracles are little more than prayers being answered. Love is the answer here."

But, I argued, "The child must defend herself."

"It is not for one to cause bodily harm to another."

"But...you *have* to defend yourself."

The Small Angel pursed her lips. "You are spiritual beings in physical bodies. You are not physical beings in spiritual bodies. You defend your body—or feel you must preserve it—as an animal instinct, part of having a body. It is what keeps the physical alive. But it does not correlate with the spiritual. If you lived on a truly spiritual plane with your body, the physical body would never be a concern. In essence, it would be cared for, nourished by the soul. Everything would operate harmoniously."

She wasn't answering me.

"You know my reply," she said, folding her hands together. "Violence breeds violence. When you strike back, you are striking yourselves. It is not God's way."

A mixture of emotions rose within me: anger, sorrow and desperation. "I'm sorry," I said, shaking my head. "But I'm not the right person for this task. If someone jumped me in an alley, I'd fight for my life...including killing, if forced to."

"It is because your physical body is more important to you than your spiritual essence. Your path will change as you pray for your enemies."

"Of course," I answered, sarcastically. "My path will change because I'll be found dead in an alley, and the poor little Korean girl will be beaten up." I grabbed the Cherub's wing. It felt like rice paper, light and thin, but it was unbending. "None of you understand!" I said. "We're put in

this body, and then told not to worry about it. None of this makes sense."

"Over the years," the Small Angel said, slipping from my grasp, "the body has become more important to you than the soul. When the soul is cared for, the body will be also. Remember this, and heed it.

"As the Archangel told you—listen to the songs of your soul," she concluded, disappearing into the horizon.

Twelve

Health and Persistence

Late April

Aweek passed, while I mulled over the messages and weakly attempted applying them. Although the messengers had stated it was a "simple task," I found it almost impossible. I blocked out any more messages, needing time to clarify them.

Finally, as before, the Call became too strong to ignore. Sitting down to pray, the Archangel immediately appeared. Thinking he would chastise me for not listening, I began to apologize. With a wave of his large hand, he dismissed my regrets.

"We knew you would not be easy when we called you. We have expected lapses."

Sighing, I felt relieved. Looking around, we were not at the familiar setting, but on a small island, surrounded by water. As before, we sat on large rocks, jutting out from the land. This time, both of us wore flowing robes. I examined

mine, delighted at the feel of the light, yellow material. The cloth glittered in the sunlight as I moved. Lifting my face to feel the warm breeze, I tasted the salty air on my tongue.

"What are you going to discuss?" I asked.

"Pain," he said. "You are concerned with your body and we want to help you overcome that. The mind controls all the pain in the body, all of the disease. In the beginning of time, when you were all one body, the body was perfect. You were one with God. When you turned from God's light, you became anxious. You are anxious without God in your lives. Anxiety brings aging, pain and disease.

"It is so simple," he said again, "to turn toward God. I keep saying—the choice is flowing with or against the current. All of you continue to swim against it, like small children trying to assert themselves. When you finally drift with the waters, you will be astonished at the simplicity, ease, and fun of the ride. That is how it is with God. Turn toward Him, and the waters will carry you."

The Archangel continued without a breath. He had much to discuss that morning. "Your bodies have a capacity to heal themselves, when they are anxiety-free. The only way to be anxiety-free is to be with God. Then, all things work perfectly. All is perfect."

I remained quiet. We discussed other matters, and I thanked him for these visits. I felt honored to be in the presence of these messengers.

"Do not feel honored," he said. "We have been with you for ages, knowing that you would eventually listen to us. We have waited thousands of years. Your time has begun." He smiled at me. "Others will hear these messages, through themselves or through others, or through the call itself."

He stressed the importance of prayer. "There are different forms of prayer. Selfless prayer is powerful. Prayer for your enemies is the strongest. Another form of prayer is Deeds. Each of your deeds is a strong message to God, imploring help for your journey. Prayer is a vehicle in reaching the Light and the Word. Listen for the Word, and your lives will become simple in God. The Word will instruct you on achieving perfection with God. You strive for perfection in your daily lives, yet it is impossible without God.

"God is perfect," the Archangel continued. "As are you in His eyes. Bring yourselves closer to the Light and you will realize this perfection. He is waiting for you with open arms, do not be afraid. It is so simple, so easy. Why don't you turn toward it?"

"I don't know," I said, frustrated. *"Why don't I?"*

"Ah," he paused, "Like small children, you want to learn on your own...and you are tempted by the darkness, thinking it is the easier path. God gave you Free Will and independence. It is an attribute He loves in you. Yet, in many cases, this independence turns you from God. And this is how it must be, but there are teachers to guide you, help you on your path. To instruct you in the correct way to the Word. Please listen to these teachers."

Thanking him again, I found myself no longer frightened of his presence; the Archangel understood my misgivings. But his visits still worried me; I did not know how to implement this knowledge, nor did I relish the responsibility.

Watching him expand his huge wings behind him, the sun reflecting off the golden color, I felt dwarfed. "You are

so majestic and powerful," I said, awestruck at my helper's size and knowledge.

"Your soul is more powerful than mine," the Archangel responded, folding his wings.

"That can't be true," I protested.

He repeated his statement but did not elaborate.

Before we ended our discussion, I noticed a flash of red on his hands. Reaching for his hand, I noticed a stigmata on his palm. "When did you get that?" I asked, touching the scar with my fingertip.

"When Christ died on the cross," he said humbly, "we all received these."

"I've never noticed them before," I said, watching a trickle of fresh blood pulse from his palm.

"You were not looking," he answered me. "Now your eyes have begun to open."

Ashamed at my selfishness, I asked. "How long will you have them?"

"Until all of you come back to Christ. Until His mission of saving you is complete. Then, our scars will be gone, and the days in Heaven will be days of joyous celebration."

"It's possible?"

The Archangel fell silent. "It is possible," he finally said, "but only with prayer. You are all One. When Jesus said, 'Love you neighbor as yourself', He truly said, 'Love your neighbor...he is yourself.' Once mankind realizes this, and cares for the poor, the ill, the sinners, and the troubled—as if they were caring for themselves—all will come to God. When you realize the pain your neighbor is experiencing is your own, your lives will change.

"You must help spread this message," he said, looking

directly at me. His blue eyes had turned darker, his tone even more formidable than ever.

"I don't want to..." I said. "How can I? People won't believe me anyway, they'll think I'm imagining this..." I swept my arms around the beach, finally returning my gaze to the Archangel. "...imaging *you*."

"If it is for the greater good," the Archangel said, "if it is for God, everything will be cared for. Place your trust in the Word of God, and leave all anxiety behind you. Go with the current of His light, and the ride will be smooth and beautiful."

The Archangel disappeared and a little cherub replaced him. I noticed that he, too, bore the stigmata on his palms. Although he bubbled with joy like the other two small angels, I had never met this fellow before.

He brought me to the soft sands of the beach. I found comfort there, sitting next to him. He bent over slightly, hovering in the air, and kissed me lightly on the cheeks. Then he laughed with delight.

"Oh," the Happy Cherub exclaimed, "I'm so glad to see you!" His eyes twinkled as he fluttered down next to me. "Or should I say," he corrected himself, "to finally have you see *me*?"

I smiled back. Apparently, he had been nearby for a long time.

He flitted back into the air, and perched on my shoulder. Turning my head to face him, I noticed his body was surrounded by a bright and brilliant yellow aura. Joy pervaded his being.

Opening his tiny fist, he extended to me another diamond. Initially, I believed it was a diamond. The sun

shone directly on the stone, and its reflection blocked my sight. Squinting, I saw that it was, in fact, a ruby. Bright, dark, glimmering and rich.

"Here is another gift," he said.

"What is it?"

"It is Persistence," he said happily. "You will need it in the face of adversity, as so many do."

"Didn't I receive patience?" I asked. I couldn't even remember anymore. I didn't reach for the stone.

"Patience is passive," he said, leaning in closer to me. "It is waiting for something. Persistence is continuing to search for fulfillment. All of you must take the gift of persistence, one which God hands out freely, to help you on your journey." He smiled infectiously. "Just take it," he said, extending his hand out further. "It is darker, because it needs to be. It is so easy to give up, so easy to stop searching, stop receiving God's word."

His tone grew somber. "That is the Devil. The Devil hates it that we are telling mankind of the gifts. The gifts have been there for the taking, but the Devil has kept you from viewing them. He showers humanity with gifts of fear, apprehension and darkness. Mankind grabs them greedily, and then the path to the Word becomes more difficult."

With that, he dropped the ruby in my hand.

"The color of this stone matches your scar," I said.

Fresh blood poured out of his stigmata.

I fell silent, wondering about this constant reminder of Christ's crucifixion.

"We, too, are persistent on our journey," he said, his smile returning. "We are here to aid you, to help you find the Christ within you. To bring you together in His light.

Our persistence is never ending, nor is God's."

Again, the Happy Cherub kissed my cheek. Even though his visit was briefer than any of the other messengers, I loved his exuberance...and missed him as he said good-bye. "Go," he said, "and do the will of God. Pray for one another as we pray for you."

He flitted away, happily humming some unknown melody. I grasped the ruby, and thought of the stigmata. How could I have been so blind not to have noticed them?

I wondered what else was in front of me that I had not seen.

Perhaps: God.

Thirteen

Faith in the Divinity

The next day, during prayer, a snake appeared to me. Surprisingly, I was not afraid. We were in the wooded area—the Forest Woman's land—but further down the river. The snake carried a piece of paper in his mouth. Reaching down, I removed it. Written on the paper, in large, lush calligraphy, was the word: Health.

The snake did not explain, nor did I understand. He slithered away, disappearing into the grass.

Soon after, the Archangel appeared. Surrounding him were smaller cherubs, none of whom I recognized. He invited me to sit by the stream.

The Archangel turned and said, "You must work on your Faith."

"I know," I agreed, digging my bare feet into the grass. "But it's easier to say than to do."

"You can access us," he said. "You know that, but your faith fails you. All of you can access angels to aid others."

Without needing to ask, I understood. His words didn't surprise me. The other day, when I heard a friend of mine was sick, I called to the Archangel. I implored him to visit her, comfort her. As I called, the Archangel loomed above me and within me. His wingspan encompassed my dining room.

I felt a tremendous amount of power emanating from him. "We will intercede for you," he had said. Strangely, I felt as if I gave him some—or a portion—of his power. My own body felt energized. The minute I began to doubt the experience, the Archangel retreated.

Now, the Archangel's voice sounded soft. "'Your faith can move mountains,' Our Lord said. None of you realize this. Your faith is your power. When you truly believe in your faith, miracles will occur on a daily basis. You have the divinity within you, but you do not know how to access it. It can be accessed as simply as believing in your faith. To understand this, think of yourselves as computers, with the powers to do amazing things. But you must know how to operate the machine.

"You do not even begin to access what God has given you. Your spirit is powerful, your senses are powerful. But your faith must bring these powers into being."

"How do I get that access?" I asked, tugging at a blade of grass.

"You must pray for faith. Pray for faith for yourselves and your brothers."

I was puzzled.

The Archangel continued. "This is an important lesson—you do not realize your own divinity. You are children of God, with the same divinity flowing through you.

As your own children are the flesh and blood of you, so are you the divinity of God. You must believe in Him and in this gift He has given you. Faith is Powerful. Prayer is Powerful. Together they are unstoppable. Their energy is beyond your mental grasp. You are able to perform amazing tasks in the name of God.

"Please," he implored, "Do not forget to pray. Call upon us, and we will intercede. We are messengers of God. We will help you, and implore your needs to Him."

It was so much to comprehend. The way I understood it, inside of me, miracles were ready to happen...if only I had faith.

"Yes," he agreed.

"And to accomplish this, we must *believe* in this divinity?"

"Yes," he said, with a sigh. "We have explained the simplicity of this path, but you do not listen. It is not difficult, but everyone makes it so. Power surges within you. Faith will release this power and unleash it to the world. Miracles will occur." He paused, "All of you have trouble with faith. We shake our heads in disbelief, but it is a human condition. You believe in what you see, and semi-believe in the rest. The most powerful and most apparent, God and the Divine, seem hidden to you.

"Pray for your faith and the faith of your brothers. With this faith, with this divinity, all things are possible. Mountains will move, miracles will occur, love will flourish."

Now, I sighed. "What you say is lovely, but consistent faith was very difficult. And the faith that you're describing—sending angels to people—seems crazy."

"What is crazy?" he asked. "Just because something cannot be seen, it does not exist? When physicians dissect a

brain, do they see thoughts? Do they see heartache? No, but does that mean such things do not exist? Can a doctor view your kindness? No, he sees a body similar to your neighbor's. Love can be felt, but it cannot be located within your body. Yet, is it not real? These are occurrences of faith."

Even though I fought against his reasoning—because his arguments were foreign—somewhere, deep within me, they never failed to strike a chord. Again, I told him that I could not share this message with anyone. By now, I had recorded dozens of pages, but shared it with no one.

"Our world," the Archangel said, "is the divine. We are trying to help you view it. Once you see it, it will encompass you, and you will have access to God, to miracles, to enlightenment.

"Your soul will soar."

I sat quietly and listened.

"Please do not disregard these messages. Eventually, you will understand their importance. They will bring you to a higher level of learning, your power will be strong, through the power of God. All things are possible through the Lord Jesus Christ."

"Thank you, " I said. For the first time in a while, I was at a loss for words. I feared the application of the knowledge. The Archangel was right. I needed to pray for faith. Even with these messages occurring, I had a hard time believing. Doubts sprang up—they picked the wrong person.

Surely, I'd be excommunicated from the Catholic Church for believing in some of these doctrines.

And yet, I feared...even more....not believing in them.

Fourteen

"Each Step Toward God is Monumental"

Early May

A s I prayed, my mind blurred past the streets of London, and down through the bookstore. This day, I noticed that the bookstore was almost totally empty, except for a few cardboard boxes tied with string. Even as I walked into the library—the room filled with people's lives—I saw that many of the books had disappeared.

Without needing to be told, I understood. Throughout these visitations, I had absorbed a portion of knowledge. Knowledge of living, knowledge of understanding people's journeys. It should have made me feel peaceful, but it didn't. Understanding was one aspect; application was an entirely different task.

As the Archangel and I sat on the rock, I explained these

concerns. "Just recently," I said, "I read about a mother who forced her child into prostitution, in order that the mother could buy drugs with the money. How..." I implored the Archangel, "am I suppose to think *she is a part of me?* That mother seems so hopeless, so evil... how can I pray for her?"

I began to cry. The tears sprang not from fear, but from true sorrow. I cried not only for the child and my own inability to pray for her mother, but—surprisingly—for the woman's horrible existence. It seemed so devoid of goodness.

"Now you understand the pain of God," the Archangel said. "How sad it is for Him when people turn away. Yet, He does not give up, nor should you. You must remember that faith in God will move mountains. We have told you this before."

I knew it sounded egotistical, but this Archangel knew my faults anyway. "If *I* couldn't find enough love to follow God's word," I asked, "then what about that mother? She'll never be able to turn toward God."

The Archangel smiled, and touched my hand. His smooth fingers felt like flower petals against my skin. "We cannot repeat how simple it is, when you believe and trust in God. All anxiety is gone, all fear is gone. Jesus could move mountains with His faith. So can each of you. It is God's faith that will make miracles occur. And this faith is granted through prayer. We are praying for you, as are others. No one is lost."

He said other things to me, and I asked him—as I usually did—to help me remember them. But, somehow I can't recall it. Yet, I remember quite clearly, crying again. The same, sad, bittersweet tears.

"I'm so scared, I'll never be able to live these messages."

Knowingly, the Archangel nodded. "It is a long journey, and you have just opened the window and inhaled the fresh air. Soon, you will go outside and be immersed in it. The journey will come easily, and you will accept it.

"You are all one," he told me again. "When you see the mother on drugs, she is you. You must pray for her, and in the process, your soul and hers will be redeemed. Faith and Prayer together perform miracles. You must open up to these messages. Christ performed miracles; they were faith in God being applied.

"Christ spoke of miracles performed in God's name. Believe in God. Trust in Him wholly and wondrous things will occur. Souls will be saved, turned back to God. All of these occurrences will happen when you love one another."

Then he spoke directly about my personal journey. "We have seen a change in your attitude," he said kindly. His words reminded me of the Heavenly Woman's. "Now," he continued, "when you see people filled with anger, you recognize the emptiness of it."

"Maybe," I said halfheartedly. I almost hated to admit that he was right. Yet, recently, I had found myself viewing people differently. When I saw people filled with anger, revenge or hate, I knew their energy was being used up wastefully. I knew that their lives should be occupied with higher, sweeter, goals. "But it's easier to recognize other people's faults," I said. "I still get angry and harbor feelings of revenge. When I'm wronged, I still want to 'get even.'"

He agreed with me. "But, those feelings are not as strong as before. We have witnessed a transformation in you. Instead of harboring hate, you are letting it go more quickly.

You are not letting the hate consume you. We are pleased with this progress."

"It's so small," I said weakly.

"Each step toward God is monumental."

I thanked him.

"It is our mission," he said.

"Oh," I said. As we sat on the rock, the sun was just beginning to set, and we were quiet. Finally, I broke the silence. I told the Archangel my fears. "I still have a very hard time with these visits; what will the end result be? Why am I such a slow learner?" And of course, the question whether this was real, or was I losing my mind?

"It is real," he said quite emphatically. "It is for the greater good. We know that sometimes this still concerns you. You may validate these messages with anyone in the Church. They are messages to make the world a better place, to lead you to Christ. They are messages that will help turn all souls toward God. Toward the light."

"But," I protested, "you don't discuss the individual's salvation much."

"The individual is One," he said. "You are one. When you become angry with one another, you are angry with yourselves. When you love one another, you love yourselves. All sin would be gone, if you would realize this. No one would sin against themselves."

"People do though," I argued, thinking of the mental and physical harm some people inflict on themselves.

"Because they are in darkness. They are not in God's light. When the light shines on them, all thoughts and deeds of sin will vanish. You must pray for the redemption of souls, as we pray."

I wondered at God's patience. Because with each step forward, I felt as if I were taking two backward.

The Archangel smiled graciously, answering my thoughts. "But the pathway which you walk is being moved toward God, unbeknownst to you and your neighbors. The pathway is being moved through prayer and faith.

"Keep turning toward God. We are there for you, as for everyone. Your faith will move the obstacles. You are like children, with no idea of the capacity you hold within. At some point, you stopped wondering and with that, stopped truly believing.

"God is with you," the Archangel said. "Be with God."

"Thank you," I said. I felt terribly spent inside, as if I had been crying all morning. But, I had only cried briefly on the rock. My body felt as though there had been a catharsis.

Before leaving, the Archangel made the sign of the cross on my forehead. I saw his stigmata once again, and suddenly thought about true patience. They have carried that stigmata for 2,000 years, and still the Archangel is loving to me. I realized I was far from the path, far from living the messages. I felt like an infant on this winding journey.

I heard the Archangel call to me, but I could not see him. "You are an infant, ready to move on. We have been waiting for centuries."

I felt honored, but I knew he had been waiting for each of us.

Fifteen

"Love Is The Strongest Energy"

The next day, my mind tumbled down a different route,
I found myself on a beautiful mountain which
overlooked a vast valley of green. The Archangel sat
patiently at the mountain's peak, and beckoned to me.
Immediately, I was at his side.

He told me what I already knew in my heart. "Our
meetings are coming to an end. We will have only a few
more. You have been told many answers."

I cried softly. "What good are these answers," I asked,
"When I don't even know the questions?" My fears overtook
me...I didn't think I was capable of living out the messages.

The Archangel held my hand. His fingers, with their
smooth, velvety touch calmed me. The stigmata on his palms
glowed vivid and deep.

"Of course you are capable," he said gently. "You will
find it difficult, but not impossible." He waved his hand
across the countryside. "What do you see?" he asked.

I saw colors, all different colors, semi-transparent and pulsating. It appeared as if the earth, and its colors, were breathing.

"This is a gift for you," he said. "These are the auras of life, of people. Initially, you will only sense a color. By noting that color, you will react more quickly toward the person. At some point, you will actually see the colors which surround their bodies."

"What purpose does that serve?"

"Different people emit different colors. Their energy fields radiate differently. Through observing these fields, you will be able to understand their spiritual and physical path more deeply. When you view murky colors, you will need to pray more fervently. Always take care."

"Care?" I asked.

"As I have told you before, you are energy. Energy pulsates through your body. When you give off negative energy in thoughts and actions, it returns to you. Therefore, if you are with someone with negative energy, you can get wrapped within their field, and you will be drained. Step aside, pray for them, and send them strong, pulsating energy. Your energy will be stronger.

"Love is the strongest energy." He began discussing future medical procedures, applications which would readjust people's energies, unblocking illness and disease. I didn't know how to respond, but his ideas seemed to make sense.

Looking toward the valley, I glanced at the Archangel's large, perfectly-formed feet. For the first time, I saw a stigmata there, also. I stared at the deep, blood-red scars which covered his feet.

The Archangel studied me gently.

"I'm so ashamed," I said, averting his gaze, "for never noticing it."

Without my speaking, the Archangel replied. "You are seeing more now," he said simply. "You are understanding more now."

Shaking my head, I said, "No. I still think that Heaven and Hell—and being accountable for our own salvation—are easier concepts to believe than your messages."

He eyebrows furrowed in puzzlement. "Those who are not following God's will *are* punished," he said somberly. "But not by God. By the absence of God. Do not think that those who are not of the light are enjoying their journey, no matter what you chose to believe. Because they are in a hellish journey without God. It is for mankind to help and pray for each other. To save yourselves."

Small cherubs floated by, smiling and laughing. I made a remark, but I don't recall what it was. The Archangel laughed. "That is what we enjoy about you," he said. "Your sense of humor."

"Humor?" What a strange remark.

"Life should be joyous," the Archangel said, watching the small cherubs flitting nearby. "Laughter brings you closer to that joy. God does not want mankind to be unhappy and tormented. He loves to hear the angels sing and laugh, just as He loves to hear His Children."

I suddenly realized that this Archangel had been by my side for a long, long time.

Reading my thought, the Archangel nodded. He rose from the rock, his massive stature towering over me. Bending, he kissed my forehead and disappeared into the

clouds. Two small cherubs were at his side, I noticed that they, too, wore the stigmata on their feet.

Left on the mountain peak alone, I viewed the valley. The landscape was a rich, lush green...everything looked so fresh and new. Above the land, the air pulsated with the colors which the Archangel had shown me. Bands of light colors, tinged with pinks, breathed in and out over the earth.

Often after these visits, I felt insignificant and small. But always that feeling would dissipate, with the knowledge that I mattered very much to God. That *everyone* mattered very much to God.

Strange how our lives twisted and turned. It had taken me years to allow these visits to happen, and when they ended, I knew I would miss them. Maybe that's what the Archangel meant when he said, "The pathway to God is simple." Visiting with these angels had been simpler than I could have dreamed. All the years of blocking the messages, of the terrifying dreams, the anxiety—and for what? There was no need to be afraid.

I was glad that the angels were praying for me, because it was easy to view all this objectively, but much more difficult to implement. Why does fear hold us back from living? From searching for goodness? From being in the light?

I should have been running *toward* it.

Still, I questioned and doubted. My conscious mind kept taunting me...Angels? it said, with a laugh. Would I ever see auras? Ever be able to love everyone, especially my enemies? It all seemed daunting. Yet, within my soul, I recognized the messages as true—as right. As if a lifetime void had been filled.

Sixteen

Small Deeds

Early June

I t had been a few days since I had prayed. Often, I would find the messages so overpowering, that I stepped away.

I'm sure many people would question my desire to rest from such a journey, but I needed sanity checks. Even at our Tae Kwon Do summer picnic, as I flew through the air to break a board, I thought of the Archangel. 'If someone attacked me, I'd still break his knees,' I thought, directing my internal comment to the Archangel.

But, I also knew his reply.

Finally, as before, the Call became too strong for me to ignore. Closing my eyes, I discovered that the bookstore was empty. The elderly man greeted me—encouraging me with a nod to continue down the stairs. By now, the library was almost all packed, and I felt as if the angels were moving toward someplace else, or someone else.

The Archangel appeared. We were in a valley, nestled

on the bank of river between mountains. After greeting me, the Archangel put his arm around my shoulder, and said, "It's so wonderful to see you."

I began apologizing, but he raised his hand to stop me. "We understand," he said.

Above us, a bevy of cherubs laughed. "There is much for you to understand," the Archangel continued, "and it is not always easy. We are proud of your progress."

"Progress?" I asked. I hardly felt as if I were progressing. "I'm not living the way you've instructed. I don't love all my neighbors."

He smiled kindly at me, a beautiful, understanding smile. "Ah," he said, "But you are thinking of our messages in your actions. Just thinking of them allows you to view the world differently and become a different person. You are dropping the hateful thoughts which you carried. In the back of your mind, you are realizing that you are all One. And that you must love your neighbor as yourself, because you are he."

I nodded. The concept held steady in my mind. If it were true, as I suspected, all my actions reflected on myself.

An interesting premise.

"I appreciate the gifts which surround us," I said softly. "But, I'm having a hard time applying them. Actually putting your words into practice."

Nodding, as if he already anticipated my problems without my voicing them, he said, "You must start with charitable deeds."

Almost angrily, I turned toward him. "I knew you'd say something like that. Don't you see, I'm not a saint? Or a Mother Teresa?" And, I added loudly, "neither are most people."

The Archangel smiled again. "You do not listen to my words. Have we asked you to relinquish everything for God?"

I thought he had.

"At some point," he said quietly, "You will want to. All of you will be eager to. That is the ultimate goal. But we understand that you cannot complete such an undertaking easily. There are small steps involved." He paused, and said, "Here is my message: Small Deeds."

"Small deeds? Like what?" My mind already wandered, swallowed up in the responsibilities I feared would fall onto my shoulders.

"Initially, small charitable acts. They are the first steps."

"Such as?"

"Kindness in small matters, tiny matters. If someone steps in front of you in line, instead of anger, smile. Acknowledge their presence, and your kindness, and allow them to remain."

He continued, "The same should happen if someone drives in front of your car. Wave, smile. This energy spreads. This is God's love in small gifts to the world. People will become receptive of this, and in turn, will embrace this positive energy."

"Just like that?"

"No," he said, "Not immediately. But soon the small deeds will grow in impact, and larger deeds will occur. People's mind-set will change. With this change, the doors are open for God's love, God's message, and His light to come into the world. Each small step on this path leads to God."

The Archangel made it sound so easy.

"It is easy," he agreed. "It is simple. We keep repeating that God's love is available for the taking. Your life will be free of stress when you place full confidence in this love."

"I still think I'm the wrong person." It all seemed like such a struggle, so difficult. As if he were talking to a brick wall—and I was the wall.

"We know," he said. "But we are patient. Each brick can be dismantled. We are willing to work quietly and patiently with the world. But the world must listen to our knock.

"That is part of your goal. To help them listen to this knocking," he said.

"I don't want a goal."

"We have said this before, God's will be done."

I didn't want to discuss goals or responsibilities. "Are we finished for today?" I asked.

"For today," he said. "Because it is all you are willing to hear." He raised his hand downward, and then across, making the sign of the cross. As he flew away, his majestic wings spread behind him, and silently lifted him into the sky.

I chastised myself for constantly questioning the Archangel, always being difficult. I was amazed at his steadfast patience and love. It seemed he knew me better than I knew myself, and loved me regardless. He wanted to bring me to God, and was willing to work endlessly for that purpose.

Later, as I typed, I realized that we are all to bring each other to God. We, too, need to work endlessly for that purpose. Perhaps that was what so concerned me—where was I going to find the endless love, compassion, and patience which the Archangel seemed so filled with?

114

I found myself crying silently, and felt surprised. I had been touched by the Archangel's love, much more than I realized.

Seventeen

Reflections In The Water

Mid-May

The messages were beginning to exhaust me. As I heard the calling, I felt overloaded, unworthy and terribly reluctant. Even with the stream of sessions, I still hadn't been able to apply the messages in my life...at least not in the manner the Archangel had suggested.

Closing my eyes, I entered the bookstore and found that the books were fully crated; the bookkeeper was gone.

As I descended the circular staircase, I noticed a locked glass door which I had never seen before. Peering in, I saw a street filled with bookstores of various sizes. As in an indoor arcade, the stores were covered with a transparent, glass ceiling. I twisted the doorknob, but to no avail. Turning away, I continued along my regular route.

The Archangel greeted me near the stream, at a small pool of water. Before starting the session, I said, "I saw a street of bookstores..."

"There are thousands of lessons you have yet to learn," he interrupted. "Their time will come, but it is not now. You must first fully participate in the messages which have been given to you."

I sighed.

Touching my shoulder, he asked me to look into water. I bent down and saw our reflections in the still, blue liquid. I appeared small next to the Archangel's illuminating presence. I straightened up and sat back. Obviously, I was no longer able to see our reflections.

"God, like this water, is still and waiting," the Archangel said, standing close to the shore, his feet almost touching the cool water. "If you face God, He will be reflected within you, but if you do not face Him, you will not absorb His love nor see Him. You must face the Lord, be willing to lose yourself in His stillness, become lost in His love."

I pondered it. It seemed simple.

Something has been bothering me, I told the Archangel. "I've been having nightmares. In them, I'm a child again, and people are treating me horribly. They seem so real, but I know these nightmares aren't true." I paused, "I'm not slipping off the edge, am I?"

"It is the Evil trying to keep you from God," the Archangel replied quite calmly.

The thought terrified me.

"If you have fears and sorrows, horrendous things to absorb your thoughts, you will dwell on them, they will bury you in their negativity. Whether they are real or imagined, the same is true. You must tell people to turn to the stillness within themselves, not to devote time to the negativity and evil which is trying to pull them from God. When your mind

is constantly absorbed with such thoughts, it drains the energy from you. You do not turn toward God. Evil Incarnate wants this, it thrives on this.

"Therefore," he continued, "You must stress, that whether the events—real or imagined—have happened to people, they are to forgive, and let the anger dissipate as they turn toward God. God's grace and light will bring them closer and closer to the stillness and the Peace which is theirs for the asking. For the taking.

"God wants such a simple act. Turn toward Him and all anxiety will be put to rest, all comfort will be bestowed, all love will be enveloping. The world focuses on the hate, the sorrow, the tears...some of which is necessary for Goodness to be enacted, but if the focus is solely on God's love, all these actions would be gone. People would turn to each other, aid each other, because they are each other."

He kissed me on both cheeks, something he had never done before; it felt like a light brushing of a gentle breeze. "I realize you are tired," he said. "We have told you much, but the message is always simple. Love each other because you are each other. Turn to God, turn toward the Light, and all anxiety and concerns will be gone. You will find true peace and true love.

"And you will find salvation.

"All things are possible through God."

He's right, I thought. I was tired, reluctant and overloaded with these messages. Every time I thought I could handle the messages, some new wrench was thrown at me. Now, the Archangel told me that the nightmares were a diversion from God's path.

Yet, no matter how often I struggled, argued, or doubted

this Archangel, something deep, deep within me told me it was Truth.

Eighteen

Charity of Thought

L preferred the meetings at the beach. This day, I sat by the Archangel's side on the large rock, listening to the crashing waves. He had been waiting for me.

As the sun streamed down to warm us, the Archangel began. "This is one of the periods in your life that you are receptive to messages." He began to point out the other episodes. "As a child," he said, "and then again, at your grandmother's death, and now. From this experience onward," he said, "you will be more open to messages. They will come more frequently, perhaps by a different method, or by different messengers. But, be no longer afraid.

"You are all one. All can serve a purpose in each other's salvation."

Many issues still troubled me. "What about my friend?" I asked. "She's sick with cancer, and her life has been filled with illness and tragedy. How is that right? How is that fair?"

"Her sickness," he said softly, "may be serving a better

good. Her sickness may not only be for her salvation, but for others. It can bring out the kindness and depth of humanity in those who help and pray for her."

"Why should she have to suffer for others?"

"*As Jesus did for you,*" he said.

The Archangel stayed on the topic. He reminded me of our friends' children. The babies were both born with glaucoma and have had numerous operations. The chance of the younger child having the condition was a million to one. But, she, too, was born with it.

"Their existence," the Archangel said, "already so short on this planet, has brought many people closer to God. They have achieved much in their short time on earth."

"But," I said, my voice rising, "their sickness—and the unfairness of it—also turns people away from God. They question why a Good God would do this to innocent babies."

The Archangel looked toward the sea. "It is the people's choice, to turn toward God, to become closer to the light. Or step away. The children are a vehicle toward God. Their presence allows people to turn toward Christ, but no one can be forced. Understand that adversity is not always as it seems. It can be joyful, in that the path to God becomes more illuminated. Each of your journeys can be so simple," he stressed. "So simple, if you see that there is always a pathway to the Lord. Seek out that pathway, don't turn toward the negative, and God will lift you on your journey."

I had little to say that day. The Archangel always answered my objections, and sometimes it was almost irritating.

He told me more. "There is Charity of Thought. We know that you are concerned with applying these lessons.

We will not overload you, nor make the tasks insurmountable, because they are truly simple. But as before, here is something which all can practice. Charity of thought.

"If you cannot actually perform the deed, think the deed. Think kindly of each other, even if it is only for a fleeting second. Soon, the thought will plant itself in your spirit. Then, it will seed, and charity of thought will become charity of deed."

I stared at him, wondering about this Archangel. He smiled at me, and told me that I must go back and read my journal. "There is much to learn, but it can be learned quickly by turning to God."

He told me about the early church. And how sacrifices were "offered up" to God. The Archangel said that such deeds must be thought of, not as sacrifices, but as joys. As pathways to God. And the journey would be effortless. "Everything becomes a prayer," he said. "And as such, prayers bring you closer to the light. The prayers help your neighbors, who are yourselves.

"Be kind to each other," he said. "Because you are each other."

He touched my hand, and I saw again the stigmata.

"I'm no saint," I told him. "And not to berate a point, but if I tell this message to anyone, they'll think I'm different from them. And I'm not."

"That is why we have picked you," he said. "We will keep you humble. You are like the others, not special. But you are willing to listen at this point in your journey. You can be a conduit for others to learn these messages."

I wasn't sure how 'willing to listen' I was.

"Do not be afraid. You have heard the messages, but you

have not learned them.

"The learning will take ages."

The Archangel looked toward the ocean and threw a pebble into it. "You cannot see the ripples it causes," he said, "because the sea itself seems overpowering. But that small pebble has made a mark on the sea, has changed its dynamics forever. Infinitely, it will change it. And so do you. A small deed, a small act of charity, a small thought of kindness, although seemingly as insignificant as a pebble in the sea, will make infinite changes in the world. Changes which will affect eternity.

"Such are the charity of thoughts, such are the acts of kindness, such are the prayers for each other. At times, we know many are distressed and overwhelmed by the powers of evil, hatred, and the seemingly insurmountable problems of life. But, each mark of love changes the world. It brings each of you closer to the Light of God."

I listened intently.

"God is waiting with open arms, patiently, and with unconditional love. You need only to turn toward Him. He is in the silence of your soul. After these messages are completed, you will enter a time of silence. There you will become one with God. Be in His presence. This is available to all, it is an act of worship. Within the silence of your soul, God is waiting, as He has been waiting for all of eternity."

"He's there now?" I asked.

"Yes," the Archangel said. "He is always with you. You must only turn toward Him. And have faith in Him. That is all that He asks. Love Him and love yourselves.

"But," he concluded, "You must listen to the soul. Give yourself time in His presence. The stillness will comfort you, not frighten you."

Exodus of the Angels

Nineteen

More Stigmata

Without the Archangel voicing it, I knew our visits were coming to an end.

"It is time to move on with your journey," he said. "We have told you many messages, and now is the time to apply them."

As he spoke, I folded my hands on my lap. Something wet touched my skin. Looking down, I saw fresh blood pouring from my hands.

Stigmata cut into both my hands.

"Where did this come from?" I asked, my hands throbbing from the pain of the deep wound. I blotted the blood with the hem of my shirt.

"You, too," he said, "have been carrying this, as have your neighbors. It is only now that you see and feel the pain which was Christ's."

A numbness ran through my hands. "How could I have missed this on my own body?" I cried.

Touching my shoulder, the Archangel reassured me. I felt a bolt of energy move through my body. He explained that he was healing me. I argued that I wasn't sick. "You were, but are no longer," he said. "You have much ahead of you, and we cannot let an illness stop you from spreading this message. You are all one."

He knew that drove me crazy.

"These messages are preparing you for your journey to God. Learn them and live them, and in the silence of the peace which ensues, you will encounter God.

"The time has come for you to continue along, in solitude, and face the Lord."

"I'm scared to go alone," I said, still staring at my scar.

"You were terrified to face this journey," he explained, "yet it has been simple. All your fears and anxiety were for naught. Such will be your journey.

"To be in solitude with God, you must cleanse your mind of all thoughts, all anxieties, and be in complete silence with God. There He will be. You will strip yourself of all but your soul. And in this solitude, you will receive more Grace, you will be in the presence of God."

"Show me how to do it," I insisted.

"It is your own journey," he said.

"Please, please help me," I said. "Didn't you say you'd help me on my journey?"

"Keep your eyes closed, and with each thought which pulsates through, dismiss it. Go deeper into your soul, don't be angry when a thought interrupts you, just dismiss it. And be one with the solitude."

I tried it. It came rather easily to me, but once I found myself in the solitude, in the darkness—a place I had never

been before—I became terrified. Immediately, I returned to the Archangel's side.

"Go alone," he said. "I have taught you your lessons. I have shown you what is essential for this leg of the journey. Your time has come to be alone with the Lord."

"Are you saying good-bye?" I swallowed hard.

"For now," he nodded.

The cherubs circled him, their faces and voice exuberant with happiness. I heard bells chiming above us.

"We are pleased with you," the Archangel said. "You have much to accomplish, but you are moving on your journey. Listen and apply the messages. Accept the gifts which are there for everyone's taking. Do not be ashamed to let others know what we have said."

"Oh, but..."

"Dismiss it," he said. "It is for the greater good."

I reached for his hand. It was warm and large; I clung to it. His stigmata looked slightly faded.

"With each person who turns toward the light," he said. "It will fade, as will yours." He kissed me gently on the forehead. He lifted up his scepter of jewels; it opened. Gems fell to the ground. "Remember, they are here for the taking. We are with you always, ready to guide, teach and protect. Only ask in the Lord's name, and we are there."

"Thank you," I said, searching for the right words. After all my arguing, I realized I would miss these visits. Terribly.

"No," he said, gently releasing my hand. "They will become faded memories. Soon your prayers will allow you to be in God's presence. Clear your mind, and greet the Lord each day. You will be as you were before the ages of time—full of love for Him. His child."

"It won't come easily," I said.

"I will repeat it again," he said, a small smile beginning to form, "the path to God is so simple. So easy. All of you hold it in your hearts, all of you have the secrets of salvation. Just look within, and see them."

The Archangel touched my forehead, and disappeared.

"Good-bye," I whispered to the empty sky.

Twenty

"Do Not Leave Me!"

Late May

I felt the need to talk to the Archangel, to discuss these messages. The bookstore was completely empty—even the crates were gone—as if my lessons had been taught.

Finding myself at the beach, I searched for him. It was a cool, beautiful day. Inhaling the salt air, I waited. The Archangel was nowhere to be found.

A Voice called my name.

"Where is the Archangel?" I asked, searching for the Voice's owner.

"He has gone from here. He wants you to delve inside yourself, answer your own questions with his messages. He is always nearby, but you must learn the messages which he left with you. The questions you have can be answered by them.

"The Archangel wants you to be in the presence of God. Go now, and be with Him."

I closed my eyes, wiping away the tears. I missed my friend desperately. Following the instruction, I tried to meditate. I blocked out everything and concentrated on my breath. But again, like months and years ago, the middle of my forehead was in pain. It hurt so much...as if a cold ice cube was resting on it. Sharp, concentrated pain.

Trying to ignore it, because I assumed it was fear, I kept going. Hadn't the Archangel said it was simple...so simple to follow God?

But the pain penetrated my head; it distracted and kept me from Him.

I succumbed to the pain. Ashamed, I tried again. Yet, the pain was constant and sharp. I knew it was trying to block me, but I couldn't get past it.

Perhaps tomorrow, I thought. If I could summon up the energy and the strength.

"Simple," the Archangel had said. "The way to God is simple."

Simple for him. I wanted to call out to the Archangel, but I knew the Voice was right. I had been given the answers. I just needed to use them.

Simple.

Twenty One

"You Are Never Alone"

Throughout my life, I had tried to ignore the messages. Now, that the Archangel had left—or at least wasn't within my sight—I wanted to hear more.

On the beach, I called out to him again. This time the beach was deserted. Storm clouds covered the sky, and a darkness descended on the beach. I heard, or more accurately, sensed, a Voice from above.

Transparent angels hovered above me, and I sought out my familiar friend, but he was not among them.

"You have the answers," said an angel. "Do not seek us out for them. Read and practice the messages. Live them."

"Wait!" I cried out. "I can't meet with God alone."

"You are always with Him," another said. "He is always waiting for you. Close your eyes and still your soul, and you will find Him. It is time for you to be in His presence. Feel His love, be with Him in the silence. There you will see your soul reflected in His love."

The angels disappeared.

I sat on the damp beach, wrapping my arms around my knees. I felt terribly alone and anxious. But this time, contrary to my earlier experiences, the anxiety wasn't from seeing the angels, it was from *not* seeing them.

Digging my toes into the sand, I closed my eyes. The terrible pain between my eyes started. It was sharp and piercing, and although I tried to block out everything, I was centering on the pain. I breathed out.

Focusing more intently, I delved deeper into the darkness. Briefly, the anxiety left me, or at least I wasn't cognizant of it, and I concentrated on the void. As thoughts entered my mind, I dismissed them, going back to the void.

I was looking for God, but saw and felt nothing but the void of darkness.

And then something happened. For a moment—I cannot even describe how fleeting it was—I felt a peace. As if something were dusted upon me, but it was so brief, so quick, that I returned to the darkness, sure that my imagination had created it.

The pain returned. I tried to ignore it, but it was piercing, and I was doubting everything. Why couldn't God just open this door and greet me?

I remembered the Archangel's words, 'that God is at the door, but it is for me to open it.'

Each day, I will try harder. Or perhaps, I will not try at all. I will relax in my faith, accept the gifts, and listen to the silence. It isn't for me to question this path. God will be on it, of that I am certain. Everything is in His hands.

Even though I have not applied all the gifts, or learned all the lessons, I know they are ours for the taking. That grace and love abound around and within us. My anxiety hasn't completely disappeared, but I realize that I am about to embark on a journey strange and wonderful.

I don't know what it is, but I know it has always been with me.

What a comforting thought.

The Beginning

Afterward

These visits occurred over a ten week span. During that time, I would pray, and then transcribe what had been discussed during the period. My conversations with the Archangel never exceeded twenty minutes, although those twenty minutes seemed like two.

As I shared this journal with others, I saw the impact of the Archangel's words. People told me that the messages have touched their lives. All kinds of small miracles have occurred since I began sharing these words. One of which was a Roman Catholic priest, an authority on angels, practically appearing on my doorstep—validating both my sanity and his belief in my story.

Since this has happened, my perception of those around me has changed. I find myself less judgmental and more compassionate toward others. Although I still do not find it "simple" as they have said, I'm finding it a little less difficult. And perhaps, that's a step? Often I think back to the passage where I was compared to an inchworm crossing eternity. I pray that my speed has moved up...just a little.

I also feel more secure transcribing words spoken by the

very first visitor—the man dressed in white robes. No longer am I confused at His identity. He said, "It is hard to penetrate the heart. I am always here, waiting to speak to you. Waiting for you to come to Me. It is not an easy journey for you, but I am always there. Tell the others to call to Me. I have not deserted them. Even the hardest of you will find me in the folds of your hearts. Call to Me. I am there."

For additional copies of

Songs of the Soul

please send:

$14.95, plus

(CT residents please add 6% sales tax)

$2.00 shipping & handling to:

 VERITAS PRESS Ltd.

P.O. Box 270735
West Hartford, CT 06127-0735